GW01460224

Spotlight Poets

TIDE OF EMOTIONS

Edited by

Chris Walton & Steve Twelvetree

First published in Great Britain in 1998 by
SPOTLIGHT POETS
1-2 Wainman Road, Woodston,
Peterborough, PE2 7BU
Telephone (01733) 230749
Fax (01733) 230751

SB ISBN 1 84070 18X

FOREWORD

As a nation of poetry writers and lovers, many of us
are still surprisingly reluctant to go out and actually
buy the books we cherish so much. Often when
searching out the work of newer and less known
authors it becomes a near impossible mission to track
down the sort of books you require. In an effort to
break away from the endless clutter of seemingly
unrelated poems from authors we know nothing or
little about; Spotlight Poets has opened up a doorway
to something quite special.

Tide Of Emotions is a collection of poems to be
cherished forever; featuring the work of twelve
captivating poets each with a selection of their very
best work. Placing that alongside their own personal
profile gives a complete feel for the way each author
works, allowing for a clearer idea of the true feelings
and reasoning behind the poems.

The poems and poets have been chosen and presented
in a complementary anthology that offers a variety of
ideals and ideas, capable of moving the heart, mind
and soul of the reader.

Chris Walton & Steve Twelvetree

CONTENTS

ANDREW BUTTON

I was born in Nottingham in 1965, am married, now live in Rugby and work in Coventry as a librarian. I gained a BA Honours Degree in Librarianship at Leeds Polytechnic in 1987.

Since the age of thirteen my sole ambition has been to be a published author. At school my literary aspirations were encouraged. At fifteen I won the school poetry competition, participated in a poetry workshop with Adrian Henri, and appeared in the subsequent anthology.

My eclectic influences include Adrian Henri, Phillip Larkin, Ray Bradbury (especially his poetic style), Roger McGough, and modern poets like Simon Armitage, Lavinia Greenlaw and Ian McMillan. My writing credits so far encompass poems in Poetry Now, Iota, Poetry Nottingham International, Reach, Raw Edge, Peace And Freedom, and various anthologies. In July 1996 I won first prize in Poetry Life's 1st Nova Poetica Open Poetry Competition.

Who do I write poetry? I feel that poetry is the literary form that allows me to express myself most effectively. The appeal to me is obvious; an art form that can say so much from visibly so little. The words on the page are merely the door to deeper depths of discovery. Conversely, I like the discipline this conciseness demands. Above all, I believe that in my writing I am exploring, sharing or mirroring experiences, observations and ideas that people can relate to, enjoy or muse upon.

Inspiration for me is diverse, ranging from personal experience, overheard conversations, and television programmes, to woodlice at the back door, or a mundane shopping list! I'm always looking for an original or quirky twist on themes like life and death, human behaviour, reality and fantasy, and the proverbial.

TAKING PENALTIES

Taking penalties in football
during sports lessons at school,
or in the park afterwards with mates,
was always popular when I was a kid.

Sometimes at breaktimes
behind the smokers
behind the *all-purpose* bike sheds,
we'd play the First-to-Miss.

In a game everyone wanted to be
the one the captain would call upon
to put a miserable frown
on the opposing team's faces.

Nothing could better the feeling
of firing that goal-seeking ball
past the futile dive of
the unluckiest player on the pitch.

A game that involved so many
could be snatched for yourself
with one deft shot in the corner,
and stardom that lasted for a week.

And, the only fear worse than
missing that important penalty,
was, when the sides were chosen,
that neither captain would want you.

WAR TORN

A Serbian shell tears
a gaping hole in the wall;
Mother writhes in pre-natal anguish.
Did I ask to be born into this?
A world of internal carnage;
from the natural agonies of birth
to this daily living death.
Through the rubble and debris
of dismembered human forms
I can see irreconcilable religions,
putrid hatreds in rancid fruition.
Karadzic's rational rhetoric
is just a beguiling foil
for the shocking savagery
of soldiers' senseless actions;
families in fragments beyond repair.
A charred hand reaching out -
the fate of misplaced hopes.
The delicate tissue of peace -
a bloody, festering laceration.
She may resent the pain I'll bring,
but this will last fleetingly
when mine shall linger interminably.
I will be purged just like the rest,
unless the hands of the west
can part the waves of mixed blood.
In this muslim womb I can quickly absorb
the racial rancour towards my race;
time-held malice staining my enemies
like a rank, indelible sweat.
Inside I await that futile moment,
when mother, my birth is our regret.

THE TRAPPINGS OF SUCCESS

Your stare is frozen with provincial anguish
as builders labour over the concrete intrusion
that will be the home of your security staff.
Through your self-effacing eyes,
this fracturing of your hard earned status quo
must seem like some crafted madness;
a threat to your neighbourhood membership,
another hole in your hopes of suburban obscurity,
another encroaching status symbol
of your husband's prominent, political prowess.
While you stand in front of the bullet-proof window
hammered into place behind sedate lounge curtains,
on the street curiosities are working animatedly
on this involuntary extension to your cosy family.
Now your punishment seems almost complete.
With little privacy and receding domestic bliss,
all that remains is the camera nestling in the hedgerow
waiting for that *goodbye kiss.*

FOOTLESS

In a moment of sheer recklessness
I decided there and then to discard
my rain-damaged brogues in
the hotel room rubbish bin.
Later, talking to fellow holiday-makers
our dinner conversation focused on
the diversity of flotsam seen in Lake Maggiore.
Petrol cans, wood, sweet and crisp wrappers,
even the water-logged carcass of a young calf.
Then somebody mentioned abandoned footwear,
and my imagination was suddenly ignited
evoking the absurd image of my
rogue brogues treading water at some
other lakeside town, forlorn and footless.

BREAKING THE SILENCE

My young niece grasps for
the words we offer
like a fledgling gymnast
reaching for the bar;
wanting to start her
lifelong routine,
and every word,
an attempted copy,
we applaud as a first.

This slow drip
of clumsy communication
tentative sentences hatching
from trainee lips,
is the ominous precursor
of that inevitable flood
of endless questions
now that the waters
of silence are breaking.

HEARSE IN THE SNOW

The hearse in the snow
drives even more slowly
than usual,
but there are no complaints
from the unhurried occupant
in the back.
Biologically, at the very least,
their journey is now complete.
Metaphorically, at best,
the shoes are off,
the future promises eternal rest.

CLEVER HANDS

In the conniving heat and dust
of another merciless Pakistani afternoon,
a young girl sits on a rickety stool
her clever hands guiding needle and thread
through standard cuts of preformed leather.

Footballs for the western world pass
through her diligent, *money-stitching* fingers:
must-haves for the ardent young supporters,
supplementing her father's meagre wages;
buying her family another week's food.

Like a circus trick, pyramids of this merchandise
line the streets as households wait expectantly
watching from crude windows and doorways
for the furtive approach of the eager subcontractor;
his beard and moustache masking a profitable grin.

She works on towards an invisible sunset.
Self-taught by the perils of touch alone,
she lacks the knowing vision of fellow workers,
cannot see the face of the smug soccer star
smirking at her from the toil of her labour.

WOODLICE

They don't threaten or inconvenience us,
and their unobtrusive reconnaissance,
and long periods of inactivity barely register,
but they are always there;
a slowly encroaching invasion
like creeping guilt.

It occurred to me that we overlook them
like the early symptoms of a disease
or the daily minutiae we disregard;
the dirt under our finger nails.

Last night, exposed by the external light,
I noticed the gang of woodlice
crowding at my back door,
flexing their antennae like poised squatters.

A domestic cliché, you'll always find woodlice
lurking in the moist underbelly
of patio slabs and floorboards,
festering composts and shadowed sheds.
In the dark, damp places
like factories of human conscience:
where their multitudes are spawned.

NEIGHBOURHOOD WATCHING

This neighbourhood behaves just like
a perfectly programmed creature of habit;
people performing regular routines robotically.
The woman at No 25 takes her daughter
for the usual 11.14 outing that always last for an hour.
The elderly couple who own the red Ford Escort
frequently go for a drive around 2 o'clock
slamming the back gate that won't shut properly.
The tall bloke at No 16 works night shifts
always leaving the house, wife and sleeping child
at 9.30ish every week day evening.
There are numerous acts of wanton carelessness too.
Like the windows left temptingly ajar,
gates and side entrances nonchalantly unsecured,
unclaimed wheelie bins still out the front,
parcels and PDSA sacks amassing on doorsteps,
and the accumulating milk bottles of the zealous
holiday makers who forgot to cancel them
confirming a revealing lack of curtain activity.
You can always tell who's got the most to lose:
the four car families (all new) and other trappings
like the six berth caravan cruiser, or the
new home entertainment centre and state-of-the-art PC
delivered by a conspicuous Comet van to No 21
On Wednesday, September 23rd at about 3.32,
the driver staying just long enough to advertise
the purchaser's enviable consumer acquisitions.
They're the ones with the obtrusive home alarms
that entice like pouting prostitutes.
The prudent few who want to keep what they've got
use their probing searchlights and vigilant pets;
the cat who sees everything from the bedroom window,
or the faithful hound whose baskerville growl is
activated within a quarter mile radius of the house.

Yes, I've been watching this neighbourhood,
and tonight with the shadows of darkness on my side,
and this tool kit of information in my head -
     I'm going to work.

THE PLASTIC GRIN

Did she wheel this pushchair
around all the shops in town?
Did she get the same furtive glances,
the same wild, runaway curiosity
that I try to rein in, now?

Her stare is direct and unwavering,
I can see no disturbing subplot
behind the main story of her questions.
There is nothing in her polite manner
to suggest a snag in the fabric of her mind.

She exchanges pleasantries with me
as she would recipes with a friend.
Even in the nature of her subject request:
Health and Diet, I can imagine
little scope for a deranged agenda.

It's just the pushchair and its contents.
The small baby silent and motionless
with a face so flawlessly smooth
set forever in a plastic grin.

THE REAL SPIRIT

In the dog-eared photograph
three elderly women, seated,
hold plastic mugs aloft
in a concerted celebration.

They really don't look as if
they've got that much
to outwardly smile about
in this insipid setting
of care home decor
with its anaemic wallpaper
and Spartan furnishings
in a colour scheme for the dying.

Despite the mental resignation,
the physical discomforts,
and the social sidelining,
the obstinate presence
of their human spirit
squats in this picture
like a photogenic ghost
with its tongue sticking out.

Of course, it could just be
that the alcoholic elixir,
already drained from their mugs,
is starting to take effect.

A DART THROWN

In that small pocket of pregnant time
between the throwing of the dart,
and the resounding thud of metal in bristle;
beds of breathing babies have been born,
funerals of fatalities gravely registered,
churches of couples have taken their vows
while courts of others have cast them aside.

During that graceful trajectory of flight
when the final outcome is still uncertain;
lunches of lucrative deals have been secured,
streets of small boys have fallen off their bikes,
races of religious wars have divided nations,
schools of Sarahs have achieved 4 As at A Level
while queues of Johns signed on for the first time.

In the charged moment of congested tension
when his opponent considers the margins of error;
one of only 16 remaining pits has already closed,
pulses of patients awoke to a new heartbeat,
unisons of unions have gone on strike again,
papers of peace may have been signed in Northern Ireland
while overdoses of addicts have tragically expired.

During that suspended ecstasy of flight
as we follow the fateful arc
of that dart's final, prized location,
more important journeys will never reach
Such a simple destination.

RUTH CALDER

I grew up in the West Midlands with my younger sister and brother. I began to write poetry when I was seven years old, and this, along with music, painting and other literature has remained amongst my main interests. I was encouraged to read poetry by my mother whilst I was at school and this helped to lay the foundations for my own poetry writing. However, it was during my A levels, which I studied at King Edward V1 sixth form college in Stourbridge, that I began to read a far wider range of styles. As a result, I was encouraged to experiment with my own approach to writing poetry. This was largely due to one of my A level English teachers, Mr C A Spicer, who introduced me to poets such as Emily Dickinson and W B Yeats. Having passed my A levels I went to Bangor University in North Wales and completed a degree in music. Whilst living there I also renewed my interest in mountain walking. After training in Bangor as a secondary school music and English teacher, I moved to the North Pennines where I obtained a post as music teacher in Lochinvar School, and Samuel King's School where I also teach English. Since living in Cumbria I have been encouraged in reading and writing poetry by my friend and fellow poet Russell Bowley. Amongst the published poets who have influenced me are W B Yeats, Emily Dickinson and G M Hopkins.

QUICKSAND

Again I hear the footsteps
upon my silent soul
that echo to eternity
and tread from pole to pole.
They chart my every movement
from bloodshed at my birth
to the sequestered future when
my dust returns to earth.
They pulse through all the seasons,
they thunder in my thought
and rhythmic send my throbbing heart
to where its life was wrought.
When suddenly the silence
engulfs me like a sea.
I slip into the sinking sand
that slowly swallows me.

SHOOTING STARS

Thoughts buzz like flies
around the stagnation
of my mind -
Gems in a mire.
Like shooting stars in a
midnight sky
they fade and die
in the black hole
of my brain.
Stifled in the
sinking sands of my
existence,
Starved and smothered,
spark their
electric last.

MOLES

Hung up to dry
in the pearly winter white
of the new day
like so much black washing
on Death's barbed line.
Nine velveteen
frozen forms,
neat as an undertaker's
chess board.
Sharps and flats
placed perfect
in a silent scale.
Here you hang.
Ebony in the
snow-soft
sonata of the world.

QUICKENING

The whirlwind awakes.
Thunder like Thor's hammer
lightning quick
like the light,
bright silver
of mercury in my veins
dances me into
a burning ecstasy
of being.

ANOREXIA

Imprisoned
in the empty cage
of myself
I drift.
Mind crazed,
fly
frenzied
to the giddy heights -
spiral to the depths
of the insane inferno
in the withered heart of

I.

My body
dry bones dancing
hunger defying
sparks brilliance
to my brain
like stars in the black abyss.
Sharp and bright as a knife edge
the pain razors silver
into my heart.
There the genius of folly
shoots
to kill.

THE ROOKS

A thunder cloud
the midnight crowd
converge.
Black as whirlwind's
inner eye,
drawn magnetic
from the day-bright heavens,
the scavengers settle
restless.
Seasonal rite and
season's rights
perform,
flung outwards like
tarmac-black leaves
from the stripped naked tree
to return,
instinctive to its
telepathic touch.

THE MADNESS

Don't question me
when madness
takes my spirit
spiralling to
silent spectres' dark abode.
Don't speak to me
of sanity
and calm my mind
for medicine and sanctity.
Don't stop my soaring ecstasy
to heaven's high
eternal dome,
but watch me rise
upon the winds
of sighs and
silent words.
There if you will,
my fire see
and know
this madness
burns in me.

KNIFE EDGE

In the white fragility
delicate life lines
beckon to be broken.
Blue and beautiful
keep time
for the sonata of my life.
Hypnotic,
draw me into themselves
which are myself
and offer their
ruby warmth
for my death bed's
feather bed
comforting repose.
Sharp as citrus,
silver slips
through the mother of pearl
oyster white
strata
of my evolution.
Infant to adult
regress,
return to
womb-red beginnings.
Liberated
the crimson cascade
warm and bright
flows over the
mottled marble
of its parasitic prison.
The warmth rocks me
on a sea of pain
and ecstasy.

GHOST DANCE

A whirlwind in my soul
is dancing dark as
passion's fire,
as star-filled
velvet night
is dark and bright
and blind
and sight is clear as
silver moon in
Heaven's heart.

A whirlwind in my soul
is dancing,
dancing
round and round,
like sunbeams glancing
gold on dark
profundity of
ocean deep
and pearls in
oyster's hidden heart.

A whirlwind in my soul
is dancing dark as
passion's fire,
As devil's
trickster's tongue
is dark and bright
and brilliant
as Venus' light
within my heart.

BROWNIAN MOTION

The world is busy.
I sit and
watch the busy world,
and realise that
the world is still.
It was I who was busy
in the still, peaceful world.

The sun is shining.
My spirit
Knows its warmth and light -
they merge with me
and make me whole.
Dew drops glisten,
moist and bright,
Life encapsuled.

The world is laughing.
I sit here,
I am laughing too
as, scurrying like tiny mites
beneath the sky's infinity,
my species rush to meet their needs . . .
Whilst all around their needs
are met already
in the laughing world.

NIGHT

The clouds remove,
and there
where once was endless
white on grey and sight was
blind,
the stars in velvet,
diamond set,
Adorn Night's naked neck.

The mists are gone,
and here
where phantoms reigned and
light took flight and waned in
fear,
Night enthroned is
silence-wrapped,
Darkness in diamonds draped.

Night is still,
and there
upon her breast a
diamond rests
alone.
Her face is pale and
growing wan
beneath the rising sun.

CONSOLIDATION

Winter, you are not dead nor old.
You are not the almanac's diseased remains,
the corpse of calendar's out of date days.
In your silent, frosted spirit dwells
the sum and crown of all the seasons' joy
and pain.

Winter soft, your darkened rays
are not shrunk youths grown old and grey and
failing,
but cradled in your arms they sleep
and heal.
Your hours, sequestered twilight, yield
to velvet shadows' soft caress
and know the gentle passion of their touch.

You are not the shroud that
suffocates my hopes,
the icy flow that floods my passion's fire.
You are not the frost that claims my heart,
the scythe that strikes the substance of desire.

I know you now.
Winter, who I saw unseeing, cruel,
was my illusion.,
my own fear of what I thought
I knew.
Winter, still those fears
that haunt me still.

All the seasons meet in you,
to know their essence in your own.
Your place within the seasons' restless,
turning tide is right
and true.

JUDY CLINTON

When I was a young child my mother used to read and recite poetry to me - she loved it and I picked up her enthusiasm. She also taught me, from an early age, to observe and express those observations. My father drew caricatures, painted and drew. So, I was brought up in an atmosphere that valued and encouraged expressed response. This became part of me, almost by osmosis, but writing showed itself as little more than a few minor inspirations in school compositions until the age of 18.

At that point I had what was termed 'clinical depression' and ended up in a psychiatric hospital. It was there that I discovered the release and healing power of writing poetry. The process was cathartic and allowed me to touch the deepest part of myself which was, at the time, suffering mightily.

I recovered, trained as a primary teacher, married and had two sons. There was neither the time nor inclination to write poetry for many years. My marriage breakdown and then the collapse of a partnership again pushed me into anguish of heart and soul which found its release once more in writing - both prose and poetry. During this time I came to realise the connection between the spiritual life, my desire to write and the understanding that the Spirit (God, higher self, call it what you will) could communicate with both myself and others this way.

I now write regularly as a tool to my personal growth and awareness, sharing it with friends and increasingly having my work published.
My hope is that it may encourage others to do the same.

WHO AM I?

I sit within the circuit of my mind
And wait for the circling thoughts
To slow and be still.
My mind is so cluttered by others' views
Sought by my anxious little self
That confusion reigns
And my Self is lost.
I feel I am some composite creation
Of others' views of me
And I am lost from whom I am.
Others see aspects of themselves in me
And say I am that -
And with them I become it.
And they become that of me I see in them.
What is my essence in all of this,
That which unites it all
Or lies beneath the facets of my life?
Could it be love that waits
To shine through the talents of my life?
Is it not my abilities but rather
Love that makes me who I am?

POETRY

Poems write me.

The words well up within me
And form upon the page
In spite of me.
I know I must create,
Bring forth from within me
That which life dictates,
And give it form.

GRIEF

Life beyond myself
Vibrates and is beautiful.
I watch the shadows of leaves
Dance on the shining, mossy grass
But only look, I cannot see.
I feel the warmth of the sun
Baking my bare arms,
Register it, but cannot live it.
I hear the birds singing, calling to one another,
Know that they are there, but do not rejoice.
Scent of flowers waft in the air,
My nose tells me so, but I do not savour them.
I am removed from where my body is.
No emotion connects the inner me
With the outer world.
I am suspended, unfeeling,
Except for a sense of strangeness
That sits within me
And simply is.

TO LIVE OR TO DIE?

I need my God, my light, my life
But I am disconnected.
My umbilical chord is severed -
I'm neither breathing on my own
Nor fed within the womb.
I cannot return in utero,
For a purpose I took this form
And live I must, or die.
To be still-born, potential unfulfilled?
Or to gasp, breathe, cry and howl
And embrace the life I sought?

THIS COMPLEX WEB

What is it to be human!
Who devised this complex web
Of interwoven mysteries
And to what end?
Some cruel joke it feels
To have a mind to understand
But not the wisdom to comprehend.
The mind protects,
Ensures survival of a certain kind
But it fails my soul
In higher things.
I am crucified by the mind that speaks
And yet I need it too.
What the link between soul and thought
That holds the key to Life?
Is Love the bridge,
Bestowed by Grace
On those whose mind has died
On the cross of human frailty?

LET THEM GO

Let people go,
Each to their own destiny,
Marked out in the passage of time.
Let them go, but love them.
Love their humanness, love their trying
But let them go.
Don't hold on, and hold them back by fear
For fear kills the spirit
And crushes the growth of joy
Of being children of God
And if you can do that,
You have truly loved.

GOD'S THREADS

I relate, feel I'm changed,
Evolved by combination.
Parts created, parts destroyed,
Parts conceived and forming.
I am myself but ever changing.
What is 'myself' amidst the change
What do I know as 'me'?
What essence runs within my form
Which has never changed nor won't?
Am I a strand in God's web,
A given colour I
Who stays the same, but looks not so
Because of interaction?
Are we all different threads
Weaving and interwoven,
Part of God's almighty plan
Sewn out in time and space?

SLEEPLESS NIGHT

The wind buffets and blows outside,
Nearly dawn.
First sound of birds call out
And my sleepless night is ending.
Troubled mind has tossed like the wind,
Hither and thither, back and forth
And rest has not come.
The bird-song brings me peace,
Back again to greet the day,
Hope incarnate.
Night passes and day returns,
Light flooding darkness,
A new beginning.

GOD IS

God speaks in the silence,
Whispers in the trees,
Sighs in the wind,
Shouts in the storm,
Cries in the rain
And ponders in the gloom.
He smiles in the child's face,
Laughs in the old man's eyes,
Sings in the star's voice,
Dances in the girl's feet
Works through the healer's hands,
And prays in the heart at dawn.

IDEALISM

Ideals and perfection
Drive me towards - what?
Disillusionment, despair and unhappiness.
So what the part of ideals
Of search for perfection?
For, pain though they cause,
I cannot give them up.
Perhaps like a flower turning its head to the light
But never touching the sun
I turn towards an inner light
Touching enough to bloom.

MOTHERHOOD

She made cakes,
She washed the clothes,
She did the shopping.
Week after week,
Year after year
And the children grew
Confident in that rhythm,
Trusting her to provide
As day followed night.
And she thought all she did was
Make cakes,
Wash the clothes,
Do the shopping
She did it because she loved
As God loved her
Day in, day out
Come rain or sun
And the children grew
And knew life was good.

DENY NOTHING

Deny not death
For it is life moving through time.
Deny not birth
For it is life moving through time.
Deny nothing
For it is life moving through time.
Embrace it all and love it
For it is life moving through time.

DEATH OF A GERBIL

He stood with the still animal
In his hand
And said with staring eyes,
'Gerry is dead'
And then the tears fell
And sobs wracked the body
Of the child I love
And all I could do
Was hold him and his cold little friend
And let my tears rain down too.
Nothing to say,
Just the sharing of sobbing sadness,
Mixed with disbelief
That a life much loved had
Gone forever - again.
Again and again, loved ones
Torn away,
Never to return.

UNCLUTTERED BY MY MIND

My soul burns
To be heard
But my mind has
Blocked it out.
Sleep will not come
For tormented mind
Lets me know no peace.
Oh for thought to cease
And soul to rest
Uncluttered by my mind.

THE PHOTOGRAPH

His face looks at me
From the photograph
I hold in my hand,
The face of my father
Who no longer exists,
His body gone,
Turned to ashes,
Yet the image
Of the flesh and blood I knew
Sits in my hand - and smiles,
Anger, sorrow, yearning,
All sparked by a piece of paper
Sitting in my hand.

A MOMENT IN TIME

Two gleaming swans
Float regally,
Brilliant white,
Bringing me joy as
I hang on the rusty fence,
Hood up against the wind
And wonder if they know
They are being watched,
Giving delight
By being swans
On the water,
On the first day of the year.

DEMENTIA

She was old,
Frail now,
Senses failing,
Memory fading,
Weary and frightened
But she could not voice it
For no one would hear
Her pain, her fear,
Her facing of mortality,

For fear in them
Would rise unknown,
Rebuking her as morbid,
Jollying, diminishing
The fears that rose in her.

She moved into senility,

Shut off, alone,
Talking to herself,
Imagining things not there,
Disconnecting steadily
From a world
That couldn't care.

NIGHT-TIME

Night-time has come,
Dark end of day.
Closure of acting,
Rest now I pray.

Tomorrow will wake,
Light breaking through.
Rise to the morning
And start anew.

CREATIVITY

I wake bursting with creativity,
Desire to make new
Fires within me
And roars volcano-like
Ready to erupt,
Blasting its way through
The hard-formed casing
Of long established being.
Power to boil up,
Explode through
And cast to the winds
Dust, smoke, fire and rubble
To cascade down over the sides
Of that which has been.
Flowing, moving, growing, forming,
Moving towards the lowest point,
Creating new shapes, new form,
New landscape.
What strength, what excitement,
What danger, what risk
And what joy within
As new life sits on the edge
Of formation.

SPRING

I sit motionless.
A peace enfolds me
And time stands still.
It is Spring.
I hear a blackbird sing,
And feel the early sun on my back.
I touch that place of incipient growth
Where life waits on the verge
Of exploding creation.
A long dark winter has passed -
Short days, long nights and grey skies.
A time of felt nothingness.
And now spring pops its head out again
On one of those rare, soon to retreat days.
Keen and youthful, but frightened too,
Quick to return to Mother Earth and rest awhile.
Advance and retreat like the tides of the sea,
New Life tests its ground again
Before it finally bursts forth
And knows that it is born.
So too I expand, reach out,
Then frightened, withdraw,
Each time knowing that Love, like Life
Will push forth within me
And be born.

JOHN S POYZER

I was born in Nottingham and educated locally. As a child I was a thinker. I had a talent for singing which I still enjoy. I was about 17 years old when I began to write poetry and, I've lost countless pieces of good work on scrap bits of paper.

I have no particular influences and take little notice of any rules. I believe that if poetry is to continue forward, some of us must break with the rules of tradition - how else can new/different talent breathe its own air.

If my poetry attacks the emotions - as music sometimes can - then it achieves that which I intended. I write usually to reconstruct that which is broken, to encourage - reawaken the hope in a heavy soul, to this end I endeavour to reach inside and touch the secret mind.

I have been fortunate being published twice, firstly by Arrival Press and secondly by the International Society of Poets in their anthology entitled 'A Passage In Time'.

I have written pieces for family and friends and taken several commissions from colleagues. It's a marvellous feeling when someone asks to have something written especially for themselves and then, to witness their emotions unfold. It's an accolade and a priceless privilege.

I have an appreciation for the fragile heart and a message for those who feel lost, 'Read poetry and discover the wonderful person that you are, take pride in your uniqueness' remember that the tears we cry are little gems of memories that fall like pearls upon our faces.

LIVING LIFE

can you see which way to turn
do you still have things to finish
is there much for you to learn
before time for you is gone

does your flame of enthusiasm still burn
or is it flickering to diminish
does it give you cause for concern
then what is to be done

life so precious yet so short
that has so much to give
so many things are yet untaught
but to learn we have to live

strange it is that learning takes shape
when time collides with age
and I wonder why through death's escape
we leave this life as babes

remember that this life is only one
there you have the facts
so if you want to have some fun
you'd best be quick and make some tracks

for if you leave things long enough
you may find that it's too late
for you to walk upon the earth
because time has locked the gate

FRIENDSHIP

When sorrow burns you to the bone
Which way is there to turn
Harsh words that leave you all alone
Have left you time to learn

You must teach yourself to be aware
And in the silence contemplate
For words once said are always there
And being sorry comes too late

Sorry may sound sweet to some
But it does not come with healing
The recipient knows all too well
How those words were said with feeling

Now we know what we could lose
And the lesson has been learned
We must take care with the words we choose
And protect what comes heard earned

True friendship means much more
Than those who have it know
I respect this monument we built in rock
As if we built it in the snow

If you feel that I've hurt you
There are mistakes in what you heard
To think that I would do such things
Quite frankly it's absurd

Think of the affection that we have
For one another
Why would I hurt my friend
That I consider as a brother

MEMORIES
'ESPECIALLY FOR HARRY'

Often times I'll think of you
Sometimes tears begin to flow
I know not why that death should be
Nor why you had to go

I only know that missing you
Cuts deep in every way
And the pain of it grows stronger
With every passing day

But my tears are little drops of memories
Which fill me full with pride
And I know the Lord was with me
The day I took you for a bride

And I have the little drops of memories
Tears like pearls upon my face
To remind me that our love's still strong
Though you're in a separate place

I know the Lord our God is good
And one day he will decide
To stand me in the hall of Heaven
In that space there at your side

WIFE

There will be times of heartache
When sorrow digs in deep
So think of precious memories
That are left for you to keep

Although your body pains you
With the anger of your grief
Nothing can destroy your love
Take strength in that belief

Time is but the vehicle in which
We travel for a while
It will persuade the tears to stop
When the time arrives to smile

Remember then the memories
That you were left to keep
Remember too that death is but
A vehicle while we sleep

Time will come when all will be
Resurrected to new life
Then you will be united
Once again with your sweet
Wife

CHOSEN ONE

If you were a flower you'd be
The elusive pure black rose
Or if you were a picture postcard scene
Then you'd be virgin snows

And if you were a lamplight you'd be
Seen throughout the land
For every step the Lord would take
You'd be there in his hand

You'd guide him through the world
Until his work was done
And he'd stand you in
The hall of Heaven
With every chosen one

DAYS PAST

I remember you the loving look that
Shone
In your sweet eyes
The smile upon your lovely face and
The look you couldn't disguise
And I remember too those loving things
You'd say
That there was always something new
To make each day a special day
If you could see inside this man
There is this little boy
Who has set his heart and soul on you
You are his pride and joy

CLOUDS

When your mind is full and clouded pictures
Are difficult to clear
And emotions that you ponder on of thoughts
That you hold dear
Do bother you to such extent
That you are filled with fear
Fear not for understanding is
The only thing you lack
Have courage and be strong my friend
And take a short step back
Have a look inside yourself
And to your great surprise
You'll find that you're no failure
Because you're the sort that tries

GARDEN

I wish that I could show you
Just what I feel inside
How when you walk beside me
I'm filled with so much pride

It can only be a short time now
When facsard drops its disguise
And the bud which hides a flower
Bursts to bloom we'll realise

Our love is like a garden
Where buds a million be
Displayed in endless glory
So beautiful to see

GHOSTS

All the people we have loved and lost
Are now ghosts in our memories who play
Tunes on our heart strings at great cost
To our emotions which torment us
Day after day
Just a fleeting glance that rings great bells
We have all heard it
And the story it tells
We close our eyes to shake the thought
From our head
But the memories are all there of loves
Long since dead
Spare a moment in thought
Yes you know it's true
The funny thing is we all do
But we never admit it
Do we

STAIRS

When you find yourself invaded with
Thoughts that bring despair
And your head hangs low as you find yourself
On bottom tread of stair

Think not of whys and wherefores
Nor of what ifs buts or how
But of the job of climbing stairs
And start to climb them now

Success can be yours but
You have to do - not think
Then you'll be in the swim of things
And swimmers seldom sink

LOVE IS KING

Sometimes sorrow sneaks right up
And hits us from behind
Or blatantly approaches
From the front if it's inclined

We know it can destroy us
With such devastating ease
When sorrow comes in shape or form
Of terminal disease

The one thing that it cannot touch
Is love that we all share
The hurt lives in our memories
But love is king in there

Love will always have the power
Of course it conquers all
It's the soldier of the realm
The white knight from Heaven's hall

SEVEN +

There are seven wonders of the world
And all are works of art
But an eighth most wondrous of them all
Lies within my heart
It's the feeling that I have for you
Wrapped up in hopes and dreams
A heart that's full of joyous things
And bursting at the seams.

HEAVEN

Who could tell me if there's a Heaven
And who could show me where it is
Is that place just dream or vision
Or is there proof that it exists

We have a hope wrapped in despair
Our transgression we will transcend
And truth to us it will appear
When life delivers us in the end

Then that of which we wondered
Of the pearly gates above
Shall shock us with its splendour
As we stand in awe of love

For there upon the face of angels
Shall joy be seen to smile
As they lead you to the loved ones
That you had lost awhile

PUZZLES

When you're about to ask just why
You seem to fail although you try
It is because you're all but blind
With too many thoughts to cloud your mind

Relax allow the mist to clear
And a perfect picture will appear
What puzzles you will be no more
And finally you'll know the score

FREEDOM

Tread lightly on soft ground
Which houses despair
For you know the dark thoughts
That live breeding there

And when you go in
Find a window make way
Then slowly breech darkness
With the light of the day

Invite all wondrous colours of
Sunshine to dance
And darkness will wince when
It catches a glance

For there in its midst is
The dawn of the day
When darkness had no choice but
To just go away.

MARCH ON

There are two windows in our minds
One in front and one behind
Let them not become entwined
Ere the past predict your future

WINGS OF DREAMS

Calling out my mother's name
But alas as she cannot hear me
And all my thoughts shall be in vain
Because she's nowhere near me

But thoughts continue anyway
And tears cause my eyes to well
As I walk the road through life alone
I find no place to dwell.

Nowhere's home so it may seem
And where is journey's end
Perhaps upon the wings of dreams
I can at least pretend

The course of life shall yet yield
The secrets held by time
Then shall all things be revealed
And knowledge will be mine

But upon the wings of dreams I'm blind
And mind's eye comes into play
And I find my mother's arms outstretched
There - in the dreams of day

NORMAN ROYAL

Born in Cardiff, my life has been one of art.
My first stirrings of poetry came from the wild beauty of Siberia and a temple garden in Mongolia.

After three years of writing, with over 160 poems published and on cassette, I am grateful to *Poetry Now* and the South Wales Echo's *Poets' Corner* for providing an open platform to express myself.

> Poetry is the very butterfly of life
> Breaking free over dividing fences,
> Into the garden of earthly delights
> And Heaven's hoping;
> And in order to stay free
> For everybody, it is to be held by none.

ANOTHER TIME

When you left me,
I had never seen
Your dark eyes,
Shine so bright
In leaving moments
Of the welled tear,
And moons
Of held back flood.
For you had to travel
On alone,
Without the moonbeam's light,
And forgetting words
Of Goodbye,
To see you on your way.
But there will be,
Another time my love
I know,
When the heavens
In their forgiving
Will allow
This poor mortal soul,
To meet you once again
In skies of azure blue,
Without the raindrop's reminding
To see me through the day.
A time,
When I will awaken
To a new morning
In fields of embracing dew,
Without the sorrow's shadow
Of the startled night,
To spoil my opening view.

Where the dream is never ending,
And comes in upon
Velvet cushions of air,
To gently stir
The sleeping dawn,
And the blowing summer's breeze
Lasts all winter long,
For the autumn's memories
Are only the tiny buds of spring,
To live and love
All over again,
In buttercup poems
Of petal's delight,
All within the same song.

LOVE'S QUESTIONS

Please don't ask me now
What lies,
Behind the amber light of holding eye
Or the forever moments of the frozen tear,
Because sweet moonlight
Has passed you by;
And you no longer hear,
The tinkling bells of fairies
In their resting beds of cry,
Or a dewdrop fall upon the meadow
To ask the question why,
There is no morning?
For the summer lawns of sky
Are all covered in broken angel's wings
With love's questions
To the moon and back;
And because I too, can't fly.

GENTLE BLESSINGS

I'm going to
Touch the morning
Of your smile,
To see what
Day might bring,
And kiss
The buttercup moons
Of your misty eyes,
To feel
The meadow's dew;
Gathering up
All the fallen tears
Upon your pillow,
To see if I
Can find the blue;
Setting free
Your golden hair
And primrose glows,
To awaken
The woodland fairies of spring;
And hold your hand
Into summer breezes
Upon the wings of lemon,
Until the burning leaves
Of Autumn streams.

FOREST

In my mind's eye
I was carrying you
Through the forest.
The forest of sweet forgetfulness,
To escape the burning glare
Of life's cruel run
And I was holding you
Forever closer to me,
In strong arms
As stout as oak tree branches
That finally overhang,
The shaded day and outside sun.
And for a short while
The sleeping dream of you,
Was held so ever tightly
To my beating heart and chest,
That sometimes
The missing tears would sting.
For in my deepest thoughts
And caring love,
Had I not once said
That I would protect you,
From too much opening sky
And dark falls of angel's wings.

BWLCH

There is only
white lace
upon the mountains now,
and silver
in the streams,
and a primrose face
that peeps
from behind the veil,
as morning
moves to dream,
of a lost path
through the forest ferns,
where day
was left to burn,
only sweet songs
of summers gone so soon;
all ready
to be collected
hand in hand,
in hanging baskets of light
and blackberry pickings
of harvest's moon;
leaving only
one set of footprints
now to trace,
and the bluebells
still growing wildly,
in time
for winter's grace.

GAVENNY

Slow leaning over
A drunken bridge,
My friend the moon
She sleeps.
Nightingale rests,
In mellow balm
Of evening's song,
But I feel he peeps.
And sweet scented leaves,
Of woodruff
Weaves the air,
In silent reminding sweeps.
But doesn't
Play for keeps.
As early buttercups,
In their milk white gowns
Of spangled dew,
Hold awhile the lemon light.
Of past petal shades,
Of moonbeam's smile
And happy days,
But cannot waken night.
As trickling Gavenny,
In her flowing tresses
Moves the mirror's throw,
To stir the gentle breeze.
Once more,
To meet
The pebble's play,
And morning's gaze.
Yet still the moon,
She weeps.

OCEANS OF THE DAY

How should I remember you
Now that you have gone.
Should I remember you in moonlight
When sometimes,
The moonlight is no longer there
From whence I view;
And I can only see the emptiness
Hanging out the old night,
With hardly any time at all
To beam the melted love,
Into the morning's blue?
Or should I remember you in Waterfalls
And fast running streams,
Of moments on the mountain's ridge
Tumbling to meet the new day;
When all around me is stilled
And I hear no more,
The moving breeze whispering your song
To come on home to?
And should a sweet flower's scent
Open up my heart,
To fly amongst life's garden
And touch the every minute there;
When my hours are still earthbound
Whilst yours are forever free,
And the winter shards
Of memory and missing,
Are hung on every tree
With no honey to be found,
For this your homing bee?
How then do I remember you?
I will remember you in evening's deep
And oceans of the day
When the yellow cornfields of your hair,
And sad leaving smile of sun;

Caught the dying light and last sail
To another world
Upon a silvery boat of play,
Without the cares of this one,
Yes, I will remember you best that way.

RHYTHM OF THE RAIN

In poetry
There are only
Rivers,
And streams,
And deep lakes;
And I wait
Beside them patiently,
As still
As holding embankments,
And sandy rock beds,
In order
To catch their spill.
And if too much
Moving day
Comes between us;
I will arise
In moonlight memories
Of waterfalls,
To kill
The passing tear.

CASCADES OF THE DAWN

Here it comes again!
After sweet night's rain
To haunt me;
'Cascades of the dawn'
To last
The whole day through,
Without your smile
To guide me,
Or eyes to find the blue.

Falls the dream too lightly,
To catch the rainbow's hue
And free;
'The morning's light of melody'
That brings
The rose scented flights of harmony,
Upon an angel's
Outstretched wings,
To stay.

And must I live forever?
In misty moments of the dawn
To always awaken into;
'Empty meadows of your name'
When
The shy sun of gentle reminding,
Should be
Softly peeping through to kiss,
The buttercup spills and you.

Eric Allday

I was a member of the West Riding Constabulary, seconded to the Foreign Office during the 1939-45 war and served as a staff officer with a Military Government Detachment, later with the Special Police Corps in Germany.

In 1949 I joined the Probation Service in Staffordshire and retired as a senior officer in 1976.

Since then I have been continuously employed in voluntary work with the Adult Literacy Scheme, the Lichfield Counselling Service, and since its opening in 1983, with St Giles Hospice, Whittington near Lichfield.

When I retired I intended to continue my interests in art, photography and writing but most of all I was determined to read and concentrate on 'The proper study of Mankind - man'. I had read as much as possible during my working life but it was difficult to find sufficient time to go deeply into the many aspects which interested me. Family tragedies had influenced me in my determination to find out more about life and death.

A few years after my retirement I was writing some notes when suddenly, for no apparent reason, I started to write a poem and soon realised that this would now be one of my main interests.

After years of study, prayer and meditation I began to realise like Carl Gustav Jung that I had indeed a higher self and that it was possible to experience it not merely to intellectualise it.

Having had several revelations, graciously given, my poetry began to be influenced by this enlightenment and some of my work has been published in aid of the Hospice.

I am a member of the Church's fellowship for Psychical and Spiritual Studies (CFPSS) . . . 'To Faith add Knowledge'. I also contribute to the 'Science of Thought Review' in Chichester.

A widower and a past Chairman, now Honorary member, of the City of Lichfield Probus Club I play bowls and snooker regularly. For many years I was a Rotarian and was a founder member of the local Marriage Guidance Council and Citizen's Advice Bureau.

PLANES OF EXISTENCE

Does an earth worm know the mind of Man
developed through aeons since time began?
Does Man know the minds of the wisest sages
nurtured and developed through countless ages?

Our earthly shell is but a learning process
to find the divine within if we're to progress,
far is it from easy to begin the climb
yet first steps on the ladder will be sublime.

The mind the soul the inner self divine
has with numerous shells sought to combine,
with plants with animals then with Mankind
seeking ever the hidden truth of life to find.

In the human shell 'tis but halfway there,
trials and tribulations may bring despair,
seeking to mount the first step of the ladder,
fighting the ego's stubborn barrier.

This ladder leads to unknown mansions,
attracting Man to higher expansions,
each rung he climbs must be ardently sought
each step will need courage the ego to thwart.

The end of his journey cannot be seen
yet from the Higher Self insight he will glean,
to future lives his all he must consign
to awareness of his nature divine.

THE SEASHORE

Walk along the seashore
in the twilight hours
dwarfed by the immensity
of sea and sky,
limitless stretching out
to infinity and beyond;
blue gold and silver
mingle with waves azure,
part of the Master Plan,
at one with nature
life within our grasp;
breathe and let the senses
fulfil themselves in
fellowship with the Cosmos;
insignificant though we seem
hope lies all around
'tis but a foretaste
of things to come
when we evolve
shedding bit by bit
aspects of ourselves
which are not lost
but absorbed and swallowed
in the greater whole
to become part of the
great unconscious
the infinite mind
which some call God;

Ego-self diminishes
and is lost
but *all* is gained
in our completeness.

THE PRISONER

'Men' the prisoner scornfully said
dejectedly through his tears,
'I think they're better dead.'

How had such a soul been fed
such bitterness one seldom hears,
why nourished he such hatred?

A family life divided,
tormented by mother with sneers,
of kindness he lived in dread.

Father cruelly derided,
no care given - only jeers,
in his footsteps he never would tread.

Neglectfully had he been bred,
his mind ever ridden by fears,
by brothers and sisters rejected.

'Love' was a word he'd only read,
a stranger amongst his peers,
rarely was a hand extended.

'Men' the prisoner repeated,
in the presence of his overseers,
'I think they're better dead.'

THE COSMIC WOMB

The Unmanifest
contains the seeds
of countless universes
waiting to be born;

Out of this
seeming Void
will spring
motion light sound
Life
in all its forms;

Deep within
this no-thing-ness,
this archaic space,
sleeps a power
beyond understanding,
an image maker
projecting thought
through the
cycles of Heaven;

Clouds of atoms
ebbing
flowing
swirling
changing
undying
returning
after aeons
to the *one*

The Unmanifest.

TEMPLE OF LIGHT

The invisible seed enclosed within
wants us to know we must the search begin
to seek the source of all our wisdom
in the inner realm of our heavenly kingdom.

Its home, the soul the temple of light,
holds intuitive thoughts of wrong and right,
revealing everything hitherto hidden
hoping we will do as we are bidden.

From this temple the higher self will give
authority on how we ourselves should live,
teaching us how we may heal the past,
the future with grace it will forecast.

Seek this unknown self in your temple now,
the connection surely will peace endow,
wisdom joy love courage await you there,
will help you the cross of life to bear.

REQUIEM

When you hear these words my friends
my Mind will be elsewhere,
'tis my body only rests encased
discarded after constant wear;
but thoughts of me may still remain,
lingering after my soul has left,
remembered by a very few
who of my love now feel bereft.

Yet nature tells us if we look
that earthly life is but a prelude,
a step in Cosmic evolution
and parting's just an interlude;
all death is followed by rebirth
so I beg you to take heart,
though spirit now has fled the earth
it surely has become a part
of the all-embracing firmament;
pray for my soul, my inner self,
but sorrow not, do not lament.

HOW LONG

How long dear God,
How long before we learn?
How odd, how very odd,
Though we yearn
For peace and happiness
We destroy and kill,
Project our bitterness
And impose our will;
How long to discover
The depths of our minds,
Their affinity with other
Suffering, living kinds?
How long does it take
To learn to love,
To rise for Your sake
To a Higher Self above?
How long to climb the hill
To reach the hidden mind,
Which, with our spirit, fill
The frame by You designed?

DREAM STUFF

The people in our dream
speak without a sound,
yet so real they seem
why never are they found
when daylight comes around?

The places in our dreams
are most unfamiliar,
strange Picasso scenes,
we wonder where they are
whether near or far.

Does life itself consist of dreams,
to which our mind gives birth,
what is it that man gleans
to help him here on earth,
what is their real worth?

Fantasies of the past,
dream stuff without doubt,
rarely do they last,
all common-sense they flout
though we cannot do without.

Residues of former lives
phoenixlike burst through,
Dreaming - Self then ever strives
past joys and sorrows to renew,
can such a world be really true?

When Sigmund Freud and Gustav Jung
each other analysed
conceptions new were surely flung
into a world internalised;
'Der Traum' was now immortalised.

Is dream thought and feeling
fermenting in the mind,
inexorably concealing
life of a different kind
which one day we will find

hold mysterious unknown traces
man symbolically shelves,
cocooned in atomic spaces
wherein his spirit delves
to seek his archetypal selves?

OUR TWO SELVES

This *Higher Self* shall not grow old with age,
Nor against the dying of the light rage,
Countless aeons will pass across its brow,
Yet 'tis forever present in the now
And if man allows will be a guiding light
Bearing him safely through the darkest night.

It existeth not in isolation,
All other selves are its relation,
The truth is we are one another
And rightly call each other brother;
These *Higher Selves* united are
Together linked with the distant star.

That *Lower Self* grows old with age,
Against the dying of the light will rage,
Our Guardian Self it will oppose
And contest fiercely with all those
Who seek their *Higher Self* to find
In the constant battle of the mind.

THE MELODY OF LIFE

Our body is the instrument
On which we play the melody of life,
Coming from heaven with avowed intent
To learn the symphonies of joy and strife.

The tunes we play will shape the soul,
Mingling with those lovingly embedded
From many a previous lifetime's role,
To which our fate's eternally wedded.

Sometimes we've played the trumpet loud
Next time round the delicate string,
But we're always part of a brotherly crowd
Listening to adagios of love and healing.

The music's composed as we go along,
In differing keys, in flats and sharps,
Sometimes orchestral, sometimes in song,
A big band sound is followed by harps.

And when the last movement comes around
The tunes we've played upon our gift
Evoke the spirit's inner sound
And shape the ever-immortal drift.

ASPHODEL

(Immortal flowers in Elysium)

The flowers of heaven grow
rootless in eternal summer skies
cared for by the souls of men
which dwell in Paradise.

Gently fed with thoughts sublime,
by heavenly minds provided,
their beauty is the sweeter
since they with love are tended.

The unseen perfume lingers not
as flowery scents on earth
but plays upon the senses which
to fragrant thoughts give birth.

They wither not but fade
into the cloudless sky,
and each one is renewed
by spirits pure on high.

Their perfect blooms renounce
the earthly sun and shade,
man views them in eternity
when he to rest is laid.

JOHN B KNIGHT

I was one of four children, being brought up in a Christian home by loving and devoted parents. In early childhood I was blessed with health and happiness. At the age of 17 I suffered the first of a number of mental breakdowns, later being diagnosed as schizophrenia. This was to adversely affect the next 25 years of my life, resulting in frequent re-admissions to psychiatric hospitals.

As a child, largely due to the early encouragement of my parents my interests lay mainly in music, where I learnt to play the piano, recorder and violin, and sport where my interests were mainly in tennis, table tennis and later snooker.

Educationally, I had little time for reading and found examinations and general study, including homework, a continual burden.

By nature I was rather an introvert, in contrast to my twin, an extrovert. I was shy and lacking in confidence resulting in difficulty building up relationships especially with girls.

Over my 25 year period of illness I experienced depression, isolation, a feeling of insecurity and lack of self worth. Out of this state came a very real need to express my innermost feelings centred very much on my medical condition.

At the age of 43 I got married to Vi, a Christian nurse and inherited a family of 3 teenage sons, and subsequently in the last 10 years 3 daughter-in-laws and 5 grandchildren. - My life has totally changed, centred not on self but my faith in God and His healing, and my writing has given me a new confidence in what God can do, as well as a means of encouragement to others in times of suffering and crisis, bringing them to recognise as I can show, that Jesus is the Way, the Truth and the Life.

MY DIAMOND THANKSGIVING
(For Dad and Mum - Rejoicing with you.)

Remember now those sixty years
   and all that you have shared,
Especially your family
   for whom you've loved and cared,
Just pause awhile and see God's hand
   in all that you have done,
Opening up the doors of heaven
   that hearts for Him be won;
I thank God for those memories
   so dear to me today,
Creating all that's precious
   that's in my heart to stay,
Indeed your lives of blessing
   have touched all those you know,
Nurturing a love of God
   where faith and trust do grow;
God grant that in His mercy
   as now for you we pray,

Will fill your lives with joy and peace
   in a real and lasting way,
Inspire each treasured moment
   to help your daily living,
That future days as in the past
   may voice your own thanksgiving;
How gracious is our loving God
   who made your lives be one,

You've known His presence with you
   through Jesus, His own Son,
O'er every situation
   He'll be right by your side,
Until one day He'll take you
   and then with Him abide.

A Tribute To My Mother

Where can I find the words to express
   The deepest of thanks for the love you possess;
Your love first revealed at a multiple birth
   When I followed by brother to live on this earth.

Love that was warm, and tender and true,
   Which made each experience exciting and new;
Love that so shared each step that was made
   That a sure foundation for the future was laid.

Love that experience both suffering and pain
   Yet always endured, whether sunshine or rain;
Love that encouraged when all hope seemed gone
   Still to press on, till one's best had been done.

Love that was able to meet darkness and light
   Because of a faith that saw beyond sight;
Love that transformed each day as it came
   Knowing that all was done in His name.

Oh Lord, I give thanks for one precious to you too
   For all that she's done is a reflection of you;
Filled with your grace, and your peace from above
   We bless you oh Lord, for this 'angel of love'.

A New Year Message

As the past becomes a memory
   And the old year slips away,
We give thanks for God's great goodness
   And His care for us each day;
We do not know what lies ahead
   Or what each hour will bring,
But may it fill our hearts with joy
   That we His praise may sing;

And if the road be weary
  And darkness comes our way,
May Jesus Christ, our risen Lord
  Give strength and light to stay;
That each of us may so be blessed
  By God's goodness from above,
That day by day, in every way,
  We grow in grace and love.

MARRIAGE

Making a promise to love and to care
  whatever the future may bring,
Arranging one's life in such a way
  that together God's praise we may sing;
Remember that He as Creator and Lord
  every part of our being He knows,
Reaching out to us both with arms of love
  so that daily our faith in Him grows;
Instead of our lives being full of self-will
  where God takes a very small part,
A new life of love, as led from above
  this is the way we will start;
Growing in grace and the light of God's truth
  and reading His word every day,
Each moment is Yours as a God-given gift
  to be used to your glory we pray.

In Love And Thanks

We send this birthday greeting
   To a father very dear,
To say you are more special
   With every passing year;
And as we recall memories
   Of all that's gone before,
They stir in us such thanks and praise
   That makes us love you more.

For where would I today now be
   Without your guiding hand,
Your wisdom and your patience
   That taught me how to stand;
And through the years of joy and tears
   You've been right by my side,
To strengthen and encourage
   In faith and hope abide.

So thank you Dad for all you are
   And all you mean to me,
And may this birthday be for you
   The best that it could be;
So adding to your memories
   A day that you will treasure,
Blessed by the thoughts and prayers of those
   Whose love is beyond measure.

THANK YOU

Thank you my Creator
  for giving me my life,
For times so full of blessing
  as well as times of strife;
For moments when I've felt so strong
  as well as those when weak,
For times when all is going well
  and when Your help I seek.

Thank you my Provider
  for everything You give,
For You have lived upon this earth
  and know our needs to live;
For You have seen what's in our hearts
  that gives us joy and pain,
And You alone can show the way
  eternal life to gain.

Thank You my great Healer
  for restoring mind and soul,
For taking all that's in the past
  and making my life whole;
For nothing is beyond Your power
  and so my prayer each day
Is that in Jesus' precious name
  He'll heal in just this way.

THE GIFT OF LOVE

The greatest gift that God could give
   to you and me today,
Is the gift of everlasting love
   to dwell in us each day;
For though by faith we can achieve
   and hope can take us far,
It is the love that fills our heart
   that makes us who we are.

God showed His love for you and me
   by sending us His Son,
To die a death on Calvary
   our hearts to Him be won;
And as we look to Jesus
   to see God's hidden face,
We see His love personified
   for all the human race.

We are not worthy of such love
   nor can we understand
How great the sacrifice He made
   caused by each human hand;
And yet the cross brought victory
   not dark and deep despair,
For love that does not count the cost
   is everyone's to share.

And on each anniversary
   to mark a passing year,
I thank God that His love for us
   casts out our every fear;
And may we share together
   His blessings from above,
Especially His greatest gift
   of everlasting love.

THE PATHWAY OF LIFE

When skies are blue and all is clear
   And nature beckons far and near,
The birds soar high in wondrous flight
   To capture all that's in their sight;
As rivers flow, and waters fall
   Beneath the arms of trees so tall,
We stand in awe of mountain peak
   This timeless beauty we do seek.

But sometimes all is bleak and grey
   No more we see the sunshine ray,
Its warmth is turned to bitter chill
   As storms bring fear our hearts to fill;
The mighty power of wind and rain
   Brings untold hardship, grief and pain,
How long must we endure this day
   To suffer in this gruesome way?

For Jesus came to bring new life
   To free from sin and daily strife,
To give to all the love of God
   If we would walk the path He trod;
That by our every thought and deed
   We would fulfil His will indeed,
And so bring glory to His Name
   To justify just why He came.

GOD'S PROVISION FOR TODAY

May Father God Almighty
   The source of power and love,
Enrich our hearts and lives today
   With blessings from above;
And as we seek to do His will
   And reach those lives of sin,
May Jesus, God's anointed Son
   Renew their hearts within;
We pray for God's protection
   Against all Satan's power
That we may share the victory
   Of Jesus' final hour.

May we be clothed completely
   With armour that's from God,
To withstand all the devil's schemes
   The way that Jesus trod;
May the belt of truth around our waist
   Enlighten by God's grace,
And the breastplate of all righteousness
   Be firmly in its place;
May the shield of faith protect us
   And the helmet of salvation,
While the spirit's sword and God's own word
   Will cover all creation.

THE HARVEST OF LIFE

God the great creator
  of all of life on earth,
Who brought about the seasons
  and from them brought rebirth;
Replaced the cold and wintry days
  by new life in the Spring,
And then the Summer sunshine -
  what might the Autumn bring?

We see the golden fields of grain
  so ripe for harvesting,
The trees so full of varied fruits
  old stocks replenishing;
The ground brings forth its hidden yield
  swelled by the sun and rain,
And all of nature shows God's hand
  His faithfulness again.

But man in partnership with God
  must farm the crop he's grown,
He now must reap the wheat and corn
  that long ago he's sown;
The pears and apples on the bough
  are picked and stored with care,
To meet the needs that God could see
  of mankind everywhere.

And yet there is a greater need
  for you and me today,
To welcome Jesus in our lives
  and in our hearts to stay;
That God through us may show His love
  and make the sinner whole,
So bringing near the kingdom
  the harvest of the soul.

PETER WARING

I was born on the 22 November 1939 in St Helen's Merseyside. My father was a miner and my mother came from mining stock.

I left school at fifteen having failed the 11 plus with no qualifications and commenced my working life as a miner. At the age of 18 years being dissatisfied with mining I joined the Royal Air Force where I remained for the next twelve years serving overseas in Cyprus and the Persia Gulf.

On leaving the forces by then a married man with five children I returned to mining where I remained until 1979.

At this point in my life a profound change occurred when I was registered blind. Since that time I have been unable to obtain any kind of employment.

To cope with my disability I learned to touch type and read Braille.

My interest in writing began with short stories written to entertain my grandchildren and although I have always been interested in poetry it was not until 1995 that I attempted to write a poem.

A poetry competition promoted by Groundwork Trust, an organisation which was set up by the government in 1982 to regenerate a slag heap left by Bold Colliery where I used to work.

I won the competition with my poem 'Bold Moss' which has since been published in the Millennium Commission News Letter Summer 1997. Since that time I have taken part in a multi-media production of poetry written and produced by local writers, dance and music written by St Helen's College.

My inspiration comes from the effect of industry on the environment and its effects on people's lives over the last fifty years.

I have a great interest in disability awareness and take an active part in the Coalition of Disabled People in St Helen's.

I teach Braille on a voluntary basis and derive great enjoyment from that.

My main hobbies are reading and horse racing and trying to keep pace with my eleven grandchildren who are a great source of inspiration to me.

POND GREEN WAY

Pond Green Way, just a street so drab and grey
Yet to me it stirs so many happy memories

Of sun-kissed days so happy and carefree
When children played their games in harmony

In a field of haystacks ripe with golden hue
Abuzz with children's shouts as they ran through

To play around a pond of algae green
Or just lie in summer shade of willow trees

To watch the lazy flight of dragon flies
Their wings a myriad of colours in the light

While swarms of bees droned in and out of flowers
In endless toil throughout the daylight hours

A boy with water lapping round his knees
Stood poised with net and jam jar in his hand

A frown of concentration round his eye
To catch the darting fish as they flashed by

While high above his head in clear blue sky
Skylarks sang in joy as they winged by

When evening shadows fell across the pond
Frogs in chorus croaked their evening song

The time had come for them to wend their weary way
Back home with clothes festooned with golden hay

That field and pond so green have long since gone
Now only memories still linger on

Revived once more for me as I parade
Along that drab grey street named Pond Green Way

ARMAGEDDON

Factory chimneys belch smoke into the air
To be absorbed into the atmosphere
It falls back to earth as acid rain
Pine forest scream in deadly pain

Traffic jams the roads each day
Emitting exhaust fumes which lay
Upon the lungs and burn the throat
Asthmatics gasp in agony and choke

Nuclear fall out lays land to waste
Geiger counters click at an alarming rate
It's within the permitted dose we're told
But deformed babies lie and moan

Chemical fertiliser spread upon fields
To feed our ever increasing hungry needs
Leach into rivers by the ton
Water plants and fish are quickly gone

Raw sewage poured into the sea
Comes back to haunt both you and me
Innocent bathers at seasides
Go home with a rash and stinging eyes

The giant bulk of the supertanker
Sails to another ecological disaster
Oil slicks blight the fair seashore
A thousand seabirds in death-throes groan

Aerosols used everywhere
Release their enzymes in the air
To erode the fragile ozone layer
Cancers blemish skin and flesh decays

Rainforests rapidly declining
Under the torturous hand of strip mining
In the ruthless search for gold or zinc
Another species becomes extinct

Like lemmings to the brink we race
At an ever increasing pace
We've got to stop and think much harder
Armageddon's round the corner

FRIENDS

When I was young and in my prime
It was so good to be alive
So many friends I had to meet
In pub and club or on the street

Then in my middle years I find
That through life's fate I'm going blind
My life was not so joyful then
As darkness slowly hemmed me in

It seemed that almost overnight
I'd turned into some ghostly sprite
Shunned by all who passed me by
A white caned leper ostracised

Now many years have passed away
I cope with blindness every day
It's with great sadness I recall
I hadn't many friends at all

BOLD MOSS

In the springtime of my life
Bold moss teemed with wildlife
Bulrushes grew by gentle streams
Willows bowed in summer breeze
Skylarks soared in clear blue sky
Above the heather which abound
Wild flowers growing everywhere
To hide the rabbit and the hare
A paradise to walk along
To listen to the skylark's song

In the summer of my life
The quest for coal was at its height
In the hurry and the haste
Bold moss fell victim to the race
No thought of conservation then
Just dump it anywhere, and then
The skylark's song was heard no more
In its place the hellish roar
Of ten ton trucks by night and day
Soon turned the landscape dirty grey

In the autumn of my life
Bold moss once more has come to life
With pathways close by gentle streams
The greyness slowly turns to green
With grasses whispering in the breeze
And copses of young sapling trees
Wild flowers shyly show their heads
Amid the blooming heather beds
Wildlife again begins to stir
The skylark rabbit and the hare

As the winter of my life draws near
The skylark's song again I hear
Above the murmur of the gentle stream
With grasses rustling in the breeze

The groundwork's done and soon I trust
The embryo laid down in dust
Will flourish to maturity
A paradise for all to see
A fitting ending to this story
Bold moss restored to former glory

EASTER

If you ask what Easter means to me,
I'd say a time of joy and ecstasy,
For the sacrifice that Jesus made,
Upon the cross on that fateful day,
So that all mankind could find,
Everlasting life at his father's side,
Easter is a time for us all to reflect
Upon this great gift that Jesus left,
To thank him for his sacrifice,
That gave us the chance of eternal life,

If you ask the same question of the youth of today,
Most would answer in a material way,
Easter eggs and hot cross buns,
Short break holidays in the Spanish sun,
No thought of the spiritual side of Easter Day,
It somehow got lost along the way,
In the bustle and rush of this material world,
Where God is money and faith unheard,
Respect for moral values seems sadly gone,
Because so many faces have turned from God.

ECHOES OF YESTERDAY

The scrape of a shovel on the coalhouse floor
The slamming of a closing door
The wracking cough of a dust-filled lung
The pitman's day has just begun

The rattle of cups on the canteen counter
The rise and fall of the pitmen's banter
The metallic echo of a locker door
The barefoot patter on the bath house floor

The gurgle of a bottle filling up with water
The acid sweet smell of the lamp shop's odour
The lingering scent of a last cigarette
On the air of a morning that's cold and wet

The crash of the cage coming to the surface
The men's bobbing heads as they take their places
The pungent stench of stagnant water
As the cage plummets down into inky darkness

The clickity clack of the manrider's wheels
The wall rushes past at breakneck speed
The men muffled up against the wind
Eyes streaming wet from the dust clouds' sting

Milk white bodies stripped to the waist
Crawl through gaping jaws onto the face
The roar as the cutter rips into the coal
The jet black river begins to flow

A cloud of dust rushes up the face
The men turn back down to the waist
They kneel heads bowed as if to pray
Please God send us all home safe today

THE ROLLING HILLS OF ASHTON'S GREEN

Beneath the rolling hills of Ashton's Green
Lie the playgrounds of my childhood dreams
Where as a child I roamed so happily
To play out my youthful fantasies

Those gentle slopes where towering slag heaps then
With sheets of water lapping at the rim
Red rocks of shale stood stark in silhouette
Cast grotesque shadows down the gully beds

Wild indians with war cries in their throats
Rushed headlong down the steep red dusty slopes
To join in fierce combat hand-to-hand
With Custer's fateful blue clad cavalry band

That towering rock of shale was Everest
Where Hunt and party reached that elusive crest
Brave conquerors of that mean edifice
To lay its myths and mysteries to rest

From the beach at Normandy we fought our way
In desperate battles through the fields and lanes
Of France and Germany to wrest the yoke
On Nazi tyranny from enslaved throats

So many fantasies we then played out
In joyful glee and youthful happy shout
On the playground of my childhood dreams
Beneath the rolling hills of Ashton's Green

THE PITWHEEL

The pitwheel stood foursquare against the sky
Proud symbol of the power of the mine
At its feet strong men by night and day
Descended to the depths to earn their pay
To pit their strength and skill to reach their goal
Oft' times to spill their blood upon the coal

A century or more the pitwheel stood
While round its edge communities grew strong
So proud in spirit joy and hope
To be part of the endless quest for coal
Through their valiant efforts Britain grew
Into the mighty leader of the world

Through two world wars the pitwheel stood so proud
To bring that priceless ore forth from the ground
To feed the giant factories of war
And keep the dark invader from our shore
When the war was won the need remained
To rebuild shattered industries again

For many years the pitwheel stood aloof
While miner battled owner over pay
With each victory their lives improved
And safety was the order of the day
In the face of all adversity
Those brave men won their rights in unity

Then the pitwheel's revolutions slowed
As many industries went to the wall
Britain's future hopes no longer looked
Towards the economic power of coal
So the death knell tolled upon the mine
One final battle lost and then decline

Now the mine is closed the pitwheel stands
As ramparts of a bridge on reclaimed land
Once strong men stand idle on that bridge
Despairing heads against the pitwheel spine
While round its edge communities once gay
Lie stranded in a no-man's-land of grey

THE WALL

I'm blind, yet I can see
The wall of prejudice surrounding me
I'm deaf, yet I can hear
The daily platitudes designed to keep it there
I'm dumb, yet I can shout
In protest at indifference to my plight
I'm wheelchair bound, yet I stand tall
In the fight against this insidious wall

In this great battle for our rights
A coalition has come to life
One voice for all we take the fight
For justice and equality
Forward in close harmony
To reach our goal in unity
With stout hearts so that we might
Emerge once more into the light

Able-bodied people please take heed
Help us gain our rightful needs
For some day you too may be
In need of help in adversity
No longer able to walk tall
Or see your way through life alone
If fickle hand of fate should fall
You could be living in the shadow of the wall

JANE BINGEMAN

Life for me has been an eventful journey/pilgrimage. After Dunkirk, my Mother, Brother and I had to evacuate Dover and by the time I was 10, I had lived in 7 homes. Educated at boarding schools and secretarial college, I emigrated to America for two years working as a secretary in Albany, New York State and San Francisco. I joined the WRVS for four years, and ran recreational clubs both in Germany (RAF) and Malaya (Army).

On return, I qualified as a social worker at the Universities of Liverpool and Bristol and worked in Worcestershire's Children's and Social Services Departments. Appointed Manager in 1975 to one of West Sussex's Area Social Services Departments, I served there until 1988.

In 1982 I married a Marine Engineer in the Royal Navy. He retired in 1987 and we became directors of our own Marine Services Company working in maritime archaeology, diving, salvage and towing.

While suffering from ME and recuperating on our boat in 1986, words became rhythmic and writing poetry became therapeutic. Poetry is a way of making sense of my surroundings and bringing that which was hidden into the light. Mine is mainly about an outer/inner journey, how we relate to God and each other within our environment. I'm fascinated by the discipline of expressing the truth concisely and rhythmically.

In 1996 we bought a strong sea-going boat and last year, as well as cruises to the Scilly Isles and Channel Islands, we spent seven weeks circumnavigating Britain, a memorable adventure/pilgrimage.

Carl Gustav Jung and Pierre Teilhard de Chardin are the two thinkers who have inspired me. I worship in Chichester Cathedral where I am a Steward and occasionally lead intercessions.

PILGRIMAGE

(A walk above Lochinver)

I came to find you, Lord;
Came to meet you on islands, where
holy men have lived, and where others come
to feel the sacred, beautiful places,
isolated by tides.

But
I did not find you there more than elsewhere.

You sought me on a walk;
A walk beside a river tripping and
bubbling over granite rocks and stones, peat
stained in deepening pools, slow moving in depth.

The path, at first tree-lined, shaded, enclosed,
opens brilliantly to the sun,
revealing orchids among other self-sown blooms.

We placed our feet firmly, tenderly,
in faithful, wonderful encounter,
climbing through the saddled wild hills,
our eyes drawn beyond, and upwards
to the peaks encircled in sapphire space;
we felt the cool warmth of mountain
air, beneath a sun graciously
vari-greening the granite-outcropped hills.

You brought us home, Lord; dropping to the loch's
edge, walking beside another rippling, bubbling
river, and crossing the stone, arching bridge.

Our feet have trodden a path among rivers and
mountains and sky, created through millennia.
Our footfall will never
be erased; the spirit of the
way will forever be in us.

MEDITATION ON THE MICHELANGELO 'TONDO'
(The Madonna & Child with the Infant St John,
The Sackler Gallery, Royal Academy)

I was told you were here.
I could not have found you;
at the top of the spiral stair,
You are not on the way
to anywhere.
Alone, you are the focus of
a one level amphitheatre,
encircling infinitely.

Yet your story is beyond place.
A story lived in Galilee,
sculpted in Italy, brought to
England, belonging to each one
everywhere;
a timeless story fulfilling
the past, set forever in the
present, revealing the future.

You show us the infant man who
baptised with water, offering
the dove,
bearing an olive leaf after the flood;
the dove
which is offered to the Lord for
each first born son;
the dove
with wings whispering a
soft sing-song sound of Spirit descending.

You show us the infant
man sent from God, standing
unlit on the threshold between
past and present,
witnessing the light of
a Mother and Child's love;
the child
who creates fire touching
the shadow; showing the
Way in faith, with a
hand still hidden in
unchiselled stone.

I was told you were here.
I could not have found you.

FEET

Feet curve,
forming curved print on rounded Earth.

Feet touch,
sensing earth, sand, sea, tarmac, fleece.

Feet hold
body straight, stretched for vision's ease.

Feet walk,
springing on short turf freshly mown.

Feet run,
body curved, speed of hunter poised.

Feet dance
rhythmic joy, move to timeless sound.

Feet curve,
forming curved print on rounded Earth.

HANDS

Hands pray;
pressed together imploring grace.

Hands take
the Bread, our daily nourishment.

Hands work,
holding the pen, tilling the soil, preparing food.

Hands meet
the other in open friendship.

Hands touch,
generating communion.

Hands hold
the child, cradling and protecting.

Hands pray;
pressed together imploring grace.

Hands bless,
dismissing gracefully.

WHY I WRITE POETRY

The diagnosis stunned.
The words hit a point of
pain, sharp, unremitting;
the scream created words
duelling for expression.
Words, written from dictated depths,
enfold the pain,
creating form.

THE PHOENIX

I am the phoenix, rising from
the ashes of despair.
A despair stoked in burning
conflict and fear, extinguished
by death generations ago.

Now through the ashes I rise from
your lonely grave,
observing the stone cross borne by
an angel with wind blocking wings,
and I read the silent epitaph.
Your trapped life's now framed within earth's
precisely measured snowdrop-covered space.

But now, past and present are fused,
re-generated, I arise
with wings moving in the
warmth of the sun's rays, shining through
the past's clouded shadow.

TWO GEESE
(Sinah Lake, Langstone Harbour)

Two sturdy geese in waddled dialogue
purposefully pace the distance
'twixt water's edge and high water level.
Webbed footmarks on the mud
draw straight lines of
companionship, semi-circles
of parting and meeting.

Both geese complete the course,
merge with others and congregate.
Only the imprinted image remains
. . . until flood tide.

MEDITATION ON THE ALTAR
(Chapel of St Thomas & St Edmund, Chichester Cathedral)

The World passes by, does not see;
does not see You hanging there
consciously surrendered
to the Father.

There, no pain is expressed;
just love;
and an infinite peace,
moving towards the Past
and towards the Future.

Suspended on a cross of wood You hang,
openly naked; revealing
the stark Truth: 'I know nothing' : 'I am Life'.

II

The World stands beside, does not see;
does not see You hanging there
consciously surrendered
to us.

Two mitred Bishops stand beside the Cross,
richly coped in ruby and sapphire blue,
holding crook and cross of gold, signs
of authority and power;
earthly power of man over man.

Standing tall, they look towards the people.
One face is closed and wary; the other
challenging, ready to defend
his place in life. Their message one
of smug knowledge, and greed for power.

III

But You are there, centred,
surrendered to the Father and to us,
revealing the Way and the Truth:
'I know nothing' : 'I am Life'.

THANKSGIVING

In the art of giving
thanks, I remain silent.
Words are hidden in the sight of
a sky so blue, life so vibrant,
blossom so delicate,
people so intricate.
I cannot hold, cannot own such glories.

Such awe-inspiring gifts require
answers. Am I given the sky,
the trees, the blossoms, the people?
They are; I am.

But,
for that momentary response,
that deep joy of recognition
between the one and the other,
that Communion within
the timeless moment; Lord for that
I give you thanks.

SPRING

I've walked this way before,
a week or so ago.
The bare branches told a tale of
cold, of snow and frost and bitter
wind. A tale of warmth behind
closed curtains, where artificial
light kept darkness at bay.

Today I walk the same
way, among the greening hedgerows,
the gold forsythia, and trees
delicately blossomed
white as snow, warming pink.

It happens every year, this change;
this subtle movement of Earth returning
towards the Light. And subtly too
we change to meet the new, which is
eternally the same.

CHRYSANTHEMUMS
(with their Shadow)

The winter sun shines through the
window, lights the South facing wall.
Chrysanthemums, with green oaken
leaves, and flowers blazing rich gold,
warm copper and burnished bronze
shadow their long-stemmed shape, solidly
black on the white wall. No radiant
golden centre reflects from the
shadow, but the sun shining through
the vase unites transparently.

THE NEW FERRY
(Buckie Harbour, Moray Firth)

Crab-like she sits,
her dark blunt bow-doors closed.
Windows in the centred wheelhouse
peer over, seeming to observe.
Men walk aboard, grinding tools and
paint rollers to hand. The last day's
fitting of the steel ferry begins, as
she sits at the granite quayside.

Receptive and still, she prepares
for crossings 'twixt mainland and
island, in rough seas and calm;
her shell vehicle-filled, transporting
provisions and people
moving from partings t'wards meetings.
Forging new links; forging new life.

THE TREE

I and the tree are one;
bending, bending,
Oh so close to the ground.
The relentless wind pulls,
pushes, tosses branches
which scratch the earth to the
sound of squealing roots.

I and the tree are one; with roots
Earth caressed, holding the spine straight
towards the sun's pull, while jointed
branches dance in harmony with
a soundless air.

TRAVEL BY TRAIN
(Kings Cross to Chichester)

The train filled at Oxford Circus,
filled to the brim at Green Park, then
drained at Victoria.
People flowed ascending stairs, through
turbulent narrows and
spilled into the great hall.
And stood;
stood, looking up.
Solemn.
Silent.
Awaiting a message.

The board flickers;
a tributary breaks from the pool,
fast walking to the waiting train.
The train moves, filled to the
brim; drains at East Croydon;
and there is space,
swaying and bumping space,
along the single track.

JULIE GATENBY

My name is Julie Gatenby. I am thirty-two years old and I have been married to Nigel for fourteen years. We have three children, Thomas (13) Matthew (11) and Anna (8). I live in a village in West Yorkshire but originally I come from Chester-le-Street in County Durham, moving down to Yorkshire when I got married. I work three mornings a week at the local playgroup which saves me from vegetating too much at home. Being a stay at home mum tends to rot your brain and stunt your personal growth if it's for an extended length of time. I have always written poetry, stories and bits of anything and everything. I have only recently sent some of my poems and short stories off to various places and I have had some encouraging results so far. I have had five poems published which is fantastic but sadly only rejection slips for my short stories. Watch this space for I shall keep on trying. I think my love of writing stems from my love of reading. I have always and still do, read anything and everything I can get my hands on. All styles and all types of writings. I enjoy it all.

I think I write about things that mostly appeal to women. Emotional, annoying and sometimes funny everyday things. I don't write in a clever way although I often wish I could, but in a way as someone once told me, that people will understand. I think what they really meant was simple. I can live with simple because that's me, simple, no frills, no extras, just as I'm found. If my poetry comes across that way then I'm being true to myself. I hope that others may find something of interest in what I write and perhaps even, occasionally, a pause for thought.

THE BIG I AM

Listen to me, I know it all, come hear all I've got to say
I'll shout and perform for you if you'll only turn my way
Don't talk to me about colds, I've had this one for years
You cried at last night's film, well my eyes are still wet with tears
Yes it was cold today but then I've been much colder than that
I've been so freezing cold my head's frozen to my hat
Poorly, you don't know the meaning of that word
I've had this nasty virus whose name no-one's even heard
You climbed up a mountain, well there's nothing clever about that
I climbed up one even higher and climbed it with a bad back
You drank seven pints last night, well that's nothing compared to me
I drank the same plus some whisky and then a brandy or three
You got so drunk you couldn't speak without slurring your words
Well I was even drunker as my neighbours all clearly heard
I've done everything and so much better than all of you
You can't compete with me, you can't do what I do
Me, the Big I Am, the best and everybody's friend
So why am I alone again, it's the way I always seem to end.

HEAR ME

Can't you see the pain, the tears within my heart
You're hurting me each day, you're tearing me apart
Each little thoughtless word, each selfish thing you do
Kills another part of me, the part of me that loves you
My love is slowly dying of neglect and the brutal words you say
Though I love you and need you I'm not prepared to go on this way
I can't keep on giving and living this kind of life
If you continue to hurt me, I can't go on being your wife.

LET ME IN

I love you very deeply, do you love me?
Together for always that's how it's meant to be
We live together, eat together, are together every day
But I need more from this life, I need you in a different way
I need you to need me the way that I need you
I need you here beside me in everything I do
You seem to live your own life without needing me there
You keep your feelings hidden and seem unwilling to share
All that you are and everything that you want to be
You keep away hidden so that I cannot see
I want to feel all your pain as well as all your joy
I don't want picking up and putting down like some old favourite toy
Show me that you love me, show the world you care
Let me into your life, I love you and really need to share
Please do not shut me out, I cannot stand the pain
No matter who or what you are my feelings can never wane
I need you now and always, please be there for me
Let our love light up this world for everyone to see.

WHAT ARE YOU AFRAID OF

I want to talk to you and hear what you have to say
But seemingly Mother Nature didn't design you in that way
You tell me nothing except what you think I want to hear
What is it you're afraid of, what have you got to fear
Do you think I'll judge you or there'll be an obstacle in our way
If you open up freely and say all you want to say
There is nothing you can say that will change the way I feel
So open up and let me in, let's put 'us' on an even keel

ODE TO THE HUMBLE CHOCOLATE BAR

For a lovely bar of chocolate there is nothing I wouldn't do
I'd climb a mountain, sail the seas
Run a marathon on my bended knees
Anything at all if only for a taste
Of a scrummy chocolate bar far too good to waste
I'm trying to be good, cutting down on how many I eat
So I'm saving my last bar for a special treat
But it's calling my name, I can hear it quite clear
It's tempting me sorely, I'm drawing in near
This is the last bar I'll have I can hear myself reason
But hunting down chocolate is always in season
I can't deprive myself of what I like the best
So sod the diet I'm going to eat the rest
One piece, two pieces, no the whole damn bar
Then I'm off to the garage to get my stash from the car
Oh chocolate bar, oh chocolate bar how I love you so
I'm in second heaven when down my throat you go.

PEACE

I climbed to the top and what did I hear
The sound of silence
I climbed alone and I felt no fear but
The sound of silence
I climbed up high and felt the presence of God in
The sound of silence
I climbed until I could climb no more, I felt and heard
The sound of silence.

LEFT-OVER PIE . . . WHY?

We never talk together anymore
Yet you talk to others for hours
To spend time with me seems a chore
Yet with others the conversation never sours

All you give me is left-over pie
Whilst everyone else gets all of you
And I really don't know why
So what am I supposed to do

Will we ever talk again
Like we used to do before
Can we ever be like we were back then
Could our love really live once more

I don't want any more left-over pie
I need and want all of you
By now you should know the reason why
And I hope you need and want me too.

THE WAITING GAME

They will come together one day
But for now to play the game is great
The holding back the expectancy
The thrill of having to wait
Barely touching, sweetly kissing
Simmering passion, secret wishing
Passion they will never feel again
Because it's the end of the waiting game
The first time has magnificently gone
The joining of two to becoming one.

I JUST DON'T CARE ANYMORE

It's the end of another day of my life
Where I've looked after our home and loved you as a wife
Another day crammed full of all of your dreams
Where I'm forgotten and lost in life's hidden seams
I've lifted and carried and held you up high
But I've no strength left in me, I can't reach for the sky
You've drained me of energy, taken everything I've got
What little of me is left will just have to rot
I haven't the strength to remember about me
Me is now gone, there's nothing left to see
I once had a name and also a life
But it ceased to be when I became your wife
With my new name came a whole new way of living
You taking all of me whilst I did the giving
I gave you it all, everything I was or could ever be
And you took it all greedily and gave nothing back to me
I know I should fight against the tide of my life
I should fight for more of *me* instead of being just your wife
But you've ground me down slowly until I'm small and hardly
even there
And I've lost who I am and I don't have the strength to care.

I AM HERE

Hear me, feel me, see me, smell me, know me, for I am here
I'm here, I'm there, I'm everywhere, know me for I am here
You can turn away, close your eyes, pretend I'm not there but
know me for I am here
Your heart, your mind, your conscious, your soul know me for
I am here.

WHAT MORE CAN I SAY

Why do you hate me so much, why do you shrink from my touch
Why won't you let me hold you, why do you hate all that I do
Why can't you see what you do to me each day
I love you, please don't, what more can I say
I love you and need you and want you with me
Yet you always find a reason so you can't see
How much you're hurting me by pushing me away
I love you, please don't, what more can I say
It pains me to see you avoid me each day
Of how many different things you do to keep out of my way
You say that you love me but then you run far away
I love you, please don't , what more can I say
We can't live together so why do we even try
That we're no longer a couple no-one can deny
No matter what we do, we do it our separate ways
Although I love you there really is nothing left to say
It was nice knowing you, we will always keep in touch
I loved you and needed you but it was obviously too much
You needed your space to do all that you need to do
And there was nothing left over for me and for you
For this there was a high price to pay
I loved you too much what more can I say.

WHAT HAPPENED

Where has time gone to and when did we get so old
Once we were young and free and life was there to hold
It went so fast we didn't see all the years fly past
The innocence and freedom of youth that couldn't and wouldn't last
Inside there are memories of how things used to be
Of when we were young and free and life was still to be.

HELLO I'M HERE

Hello I'm here, I'm real
Let me in, speak to me
I want to join in

Hello I'm here, I do exist,
I'm in the same room,
They talk to each other but
Somehow I'm missed

Hello I'm here, I'm going to speak,
They stop, they listen
But they do not hear

Hello I'm here, but do they even know
Would anyone notice if I got up to go,
Sad to say but the truth is *no!*

THE LONG PATH TO ADULTHOOD

I've spent most of my life worrying about what folk think of me
But now I'm going to be whatever I want to be
I really don't care what they think of me starting from today
I'm going to do what I want and say what I want to say
I'm sick of all the pretending of having to tow the line
From now on I'll just be me forever and for all the time
Me, whole and as I am without any pretence
It's time I started living and got off the fence
Hello world, it's me, I've grown up at last
The cruel life of adolescence has now at last passed.

ODE TO JULIA

The memories that haunt my dreams at night are memories of times past
Of when we were young and free and time didn't go so fast
There were times we spent just talking and putting the world to rights
Times we spent getting ready for hours just to go out at night
We went to Blackpool one year, remember Charles and Di had
                                             just got wed
We spent the night partying and never went to bed
You always wore your make-up and used to make me try
You would paint my face and do my hair although I never
                                             really knew why
You see boys never noticed me not with you there at my side
You drew them like a magnet even though you never tried
We used to dance in your bedroom and sing all the new songs
We'd go out to laugh and play, time just went on and on
Sometimes we'd fight and often row about things that didn't matter
But at the time they really hurt and made me feel alone and even sadder
Did we really feel so much and so very deeply too
The world outside didn't exist there was only me and you
We've both moved on to things that are better
And time has passed with just the odd letter
Although I remember the past with joy
I know the future has much to enjoy
The past has a special place in my heart
And sometimes I'm sad that we're apart.

Now We Meet Again

'Hello' we meet, kiss and hug, glad to see each other
But you're not the person I remember as being my own dear brother
I wonder, do you recognise me or perhaps remember me when
You were going on twenty and I had just turned ten
I have this vision inside my head of how you used to be
But now you're here before me and I just cannot see
Thirty years is a long time to be without you in my life
You are now a husband and I've become a wife
We both have our own families, daughters, sons and more
We are no longer part of each other as we once were before
I'm sitting here watching you, trying to suss you out
Trying to work out who you are and what you're all about
I love you as my brother as I always have done
But this person here before me could be just anyone
You now talk with this odd voice I hardly recognise
And you seem so very old and so very worldly wise
I'm trying to reconcile the fact that you and I are the same
We are brother and sister and from the same mother we came
But somehow all this pretending doesn't alter things at all
These thirty years without you cannot be bridged at all
I'm glad you came to visit and I'll always remember this time
And probably, just occasionally we'll drop each other a line
To say hello, I miss you but I'm glad that you're not here
And for the life we had and lost I'll shed a lonely tear.

WITH FRIENDS LIKE YOU . . . !

Now I've found out what you are
And you've pushed me a bit too far
Things will never be the same
Because I'll no longer play your game
I'll dance your selfish tune no more
I won't play by your friendships law
We all bend our lives to fit your needs
But resentment and anger are all you breed
You expect everyone to bow to you
And do whatever you want them to do
Emotional blackmail is your way
To get us all your game to play
Well no more, your card's been marked
Up the wrong tree you've finally barked
Whatever closeness we had is gone
But it was never there, it was all a con
You had me where you wanted, I danced your tune so well
But your colours now shine out brightly and even I can tell
Never again will I dance to your tune or even be there for you
Just as you told me, well now I'm telling you
You won't do for me and I certainly won't do for you
So that's where we stand for now and probably always will do
You down there and me up here and never the twain shall meet
But when circumstances are beyond my control I suppose with
                                    civility I'll have to greet.

AMAR NATH CHAKRAVARTY

Each of my poems - which finally gets written - finds its words and gets formulated at its own precarious moment - the moment of poetry. Being a person of many unresolved contradictions, writing poems is not an occupation which could be my natural vocation. Nevertheless, irrespective of all problems which originate because of my countless contradictions, getting chosen by the moment of poetry is a great thrill which, in my case, prevents the cancellation of poetry on a permanent basis. In other words, my poems get written - not because of my rigour or devotion to this art-form - but because of a determination which supervenes and subordinates my being.

This submission does not conceal my passive character in this matter. It is true that such passivity can deter or drive away every word which actually gets written. If that does not happen as a matter of unquestionable certainty, it is because of my irrepressible love for the fascinating unity a poem can stand for: the unity of word-music and what may be called transcendental message. However, my love for poetry too is not a property which was acquired or won through my own strivings. This was an endowment passed on to me by my parents. Unfortunately, I failed to cultivate or develop that endowment.

Particulars of facts having great importance in a poet's personal life, may have rather poor relevance in that person's poetry. To understand a poet, one has to assess and appreciate the poetry itself. I believe, 'pure beyond' - as some philosophers and poets call it - is the world where the moment of poetry materialises itself and acquires its will and dynamism. Therefore, understanding of a poet - strictly as a creative being - demands an understanding of the poet's relationship with and responses to that pure beyond. I will be immensely honoured if my readers would care to apply the same principle in my case.

LIBERATION

As the light glittered in her eyes
I saw faith taking possession of my world . . .
And deep within my glaciers
Where the ice is hardest,
Where no one could challenge the freeze,
A warmth stole in like the ideological guerrillas . . .
And I heard the impossible words
Hurled with impossible ease:
'Death to the Status Quo . . .
On to the South we must flow' . . .
And who could say then
That one could stay back
And not flow to the Southern seas?

A trusted creature of the ice -
With my impeccable social roles -
I saw faith taking possession of my world . . .
And although the ice around me was still hard
I decided to drop each and every guard . . .
And from the timeless freeze
I then seized a date
And - as the light glittered in her eyes -
Asked her if she could read my fate . . .
And I heard the impossible words
Hurled with impossible ease . . .
For it was Spring now
And there was no staying back
From flowing to the southern seas.

FORBIDDEN LOVE

As late as the Lord's year
Nineteen eighty two
A friendship - predestined -
Grew between the two.

Just courteous, slightly warmish,
'Twas nothing new,
'Twas of course harmless,
At least in my view.

Predestined, as it was,
Soon it felt like wine,
Their hair could soon be having
A thousand leaves of vine.

I spied them from a distance,
At each the other looked,
I knew their hearts were thumping,
For Eros had them hooked.

But Eros can be cruel -
As a hawk over a dove.
Oh villainy! Oh my God!
'Twas forbidden love.

Predestined, as it was,
They would take no heed.
So the hawk came sweeping,
Till death they must bleed.

Life has limits for all,
A commoner or a king.
But true love makes you blind,
It is such a thing.

My dear friend, take heed,
Choose your darling well.
Eros could be scheming
When the hearts swell.

FROM A TRUANTS' GROUND

Being peripheral is not just
Being away from what is central.
I know this geometry well.
Being peripheral is being distant
From what truly matters
And what the heart values.

Peripheries are truants' ground
Where great purposes stand derelict
And the games miss their thrills . . .
Where the alienated and the insecure
Gather with false smiles
And look at the space beyond.

Can you hear the silenced voice?
Someone, afraid of the vagrant tangents,
Is desperately trying to reach you
From the peripheral zone . . .
Which is far from your centre,
And distanced from your heart.

Of one thing I am certain:
No periphery can ever home
The truants of my heart.

BOA CONSTRICTOR'S POWER

If I knew, if I only knew,
That there indeed is an almighty God . . .
If I knew, if I only knew,
That my prayer could be granted in life . . .
I would have prayed and prayed and prayed
So that God heard my prayer
And a little of his might was given
To make my prayer come true.

Since I know, since I have to know,
That verity must be verifiable . . .
Since I know, since I have to know
That my faiths had hopelessly failed before . . .
A boa constrictor's power
Throttles my prayer's throat
And denies that divine intervention
Which makes prayers come true.

PRIMEVAL CALL

I am a foreigner, my love,
I speak your tongue wrong -
But would you miss the point
In my ill-grammared song?

Ill-grammared and wrong, I know,
But the song isn't for all.
It is only for you, my love,
A primeval call.

A primeval call, my love,
To ring the oldest bell:
I was born to meet you
And this I must tell.

CIVILISED COMFORTS

Civilised comforts may be had
Plentifully with a gnome,
But a skylark cannot sing
Inside a comfy home.

And there's something in a lark's song,
Which I cannot define,
It has strange contradictions,
But it feels to me divine.

I cling to comforts like a worm
And I love to possess things,
But the lark uproots my worldly values
Then I hate what money brings.

Then I ignore security and caution,
And sail for uncharted seas,
I get possessed by a spectre,
And chase the wildest geese.

Of course, you get close to death -
Your boat will indeed capsize,
But if you ignore the rules of safety,
Surprises must not surprise.

You must suffer, you must bleed,
If comfort to you is a shame,
A smile soaked in blood is yours,
That is the name of the game.

A QUESTION OF AUTHORITY

Close to a sewage-opening
On a New Delhi street,
As the sun was beating down,
I met this confident rat
With a mischievous grin
And a quite contemptuous frown.

There was something regal about this rat
And I was puzzled by a voice which said:
Reality is a matter of time
And right now, as the ruling goes,
No one harbours a cat.

On that November-noon,
As the sun was beating down,
The catless street of that crowded place
Saw the reality of the rat
And his contemptuous frown.

But there rules a reality
Which isn't a matter of time,
And I saw a long way away
From the cave of non-being
A life was leaping out . . .
And the great doubter in me
Was left in no doubt
That bowing to the regal rat
Wasn't backed by any reason or rhyme
And that accepting its authority
Was an unforgivable crime.

What came from the cave of non-being
Was the authority of the cat,
And although it was a long way away,
I knew it won't be very long
Before all of us could witness
The retreat . . . the retreat . . .
The retreat of the rat.

SAYING HELLO TO YOU

Saying hello to you
Isn't as easy as you may think.
For I have to mobilise my whole being
And, finally, go beyond the brink.

Saying hello to you
Demands that I scrap the games I play,
Admit that my image of Colossus
Is just bogus and that
I am no more than clay.

Saying hello to you
Means I unmask my hidden identity,
Let you see my false claims and reveal
My struggle against that mighty non-entity.

Saying hello to you
Isn't as easy as you may think,
For it is about giving my true being
And letting the brinkmanship sink.

ONE FOUGHT

In the beginning there were words . . .
And one knows what followed:
Ideas forbidden to have shapes,
Potentials impounded by impotence,
Facts separated from functioning,
Realities barred from realisation,
Materials robbed of meaning,
Life in the void of pre-life,
All of them heard the words . . .
And they acquired the knowledge
That the great divide would collapse,
That a new scheme of things would come,
That negations would be negated,
That fulfilments will follow.

And one knows what followed:
The power that preceded the beginning
Could not silence the words anymore . . .
And the knowledge of subversion,
Waking from its coma of ignorance,
Went to the depths of the seas
And ran through the heights of the heavens.
And through the clashes and conflicts
Across the countless multiverses,
Emerged the first universe ever known,
United by the bond of the words . .
The words which were in the beginning,
Which decreed that negations would be negated
And that fulfilments will follow.

And one knows what followed;
In this relative world of ours,
The words were not absolute at all.
Death and disaster never gave in,
Clashes and conflicts continued all along,
Faithfuls were disarmed and struck down,
And the power that preceded the beginning
Seemed almighty again and again.
One witnessed confusion and doubt all around,
One wondered if the universe will ever survive,
One knew one was totally vulnerable to dust,
Yet, since the words made them heard,
One hated the void of pre-life . . .
One fought so that fulfilments could follow.

To A Creature Of Time

I won't fight your word,
You are a creature of time -
The first runner of a verse
With which I failed to rhyme.

There is a sea between us
And I am hated by the lord of the seas -
Too many locked doors between us
And I haven't found their keys.

But something in my gut tells me
That in the fullness of time,
I will cross the seas and find the keys
And with you perfectly rhyme.

THEY DARE UNCHARTED SEAS

Who could refute the arguments
Of those hair-splitting analysts?
Facts and proofs they have many -
Proudly they brandish their fists.

Humans cannot have more than
What is broken or disintegrated.
True perfection which you envision
On earth cannot be created.

Those who claim they can achieve
All they think or envision -
They are simply deaf and dumb
And obsessed with their mission.

But only they go beyond horizons
Whom we call deaf and dumb -
Only they dare uncharted seas
Which make analysts numb.

REBECCA MEE

I am 19 years old and was born in Wisbech and have lived there all my life. Poetry did not start to come into my perspective until around the age of 13, when my school drama teacher entered me for the poetry section of The Peterborough Music Festival where I obtained a Second Class certificate.

This is now my second collection of poetry published, and can be added to the many single poems published beforehand.

My real name is Rebecca. I use the pen name Ophelia Kingston in memorium of my Grandad.

At the moment I am a trainee editorial assistant and hope to eventually become an editor.

My hobbies can be classed as reading and enjoying life. I am now a member of my local writers' group. My inspirations for poetry can be listed as; life and its experiences. Without these trying to write a poem would be a difficult task.

I dedicate this collection to all who are important to me, family, friends and people who are no longer with me.

My hopes for the future? Well, that would be telling.

CUPID'S ARROW

An empty bottle of pain-killers
lies on the floor
next to a sleeping angel.

Her soft peach wrist
severed by lost innocence
hangs by her waist
decaying in the web of deceit.

She who longed for her 'knight in shining armour'
got what she didn't bargain for.
Cupid fired his arrow too soon
she was struck in the prime of her life.

She gave away her soul
as she laughed and flirted
with the devil
dining in the fires of Hell.

She knew little of love
and did not understand hurt.
Her virgin adolescent youth
was a gift to treasure.

Instead this demon of deception
played his wicked game.
Now as young blood drips
from her broken heart
he doesn't remember her name.

ANOREXIA NERVOSA

Our hearts beat in tune with one another.
I lie unborn in foetal stage
feeding from a ready-made meal
safe in my cocoon.
My eyes do not open
but I can sense the world around:
Soft.
Secure.
Sensitive to my every move . . .

But alas, I was a conception
of misplaced fate.
One night at a night-club
alcohol temptation
finds her kissing a brick wall.
No emotion is involved.
Her body fuelled by lust.

As they wipe each other's sweat
from each other's brow,
they exchange telephone numbers
knowing they are a random selection of lies.
'Until tomorrow . . .'
   And so we are not meant to be
   The one I shared my life with
   Has given up the fight.
   As I lie naked
   In the sterile arms
   Of another
   Screaming for attention
   And hungry for love
   Whilst my food source looks away.

COMFORT OF STRANGERS

They came and ate us,
These strangers of the night.
Devoured us of our dignity.
As we worked
We sold our soul to the devil.
We gave up without a fight.

Our bodies are our life,
With which we earn our keep.
Physically we block it
But mentally, never sleep:

I was only sixteen,
As I stepped foot into this world.
Dishevelled and unheard of.
Childlike face lit under a nuclear light.
Look into my eyes,
I'm just a little girl.
Still frightened of the night:
Still standing in the light.

DEER WATCHING

I dance amongst the bracken
sharing my breath with serenity
taking in the silence:
This place
A wooded fortress of the untouched:
Timmy sniffs the leaf-filled air
catching venison upon his nose.

With him I stop and watch the distance
and deer enter my vision.
They step into my frustration:
I am not close enough.
Yet I sense the shyness of these mammals.
Timmy and I sit and watch/sniff, and together
we share our solstice.

TEARFUL MOON

You walk along the path
Crushing weeds beneath your feet.
Not looking at the winos
Trying to get some sleep.

Living on the dark side
Crying tears of ice
Sharing loneliness with isolation
Boxed-up in cardboard concentration.

Lying crushed on derelict benches
Under yesterday's news
Too old to cry for lost times
They leave that to the moon.

The moon it watches all of us,
The moon has seen it all.
It sits there in eternity
Waiting for tears to fall.

WATER BABIES

Splash happy in their bath water
Cleansing off their daily play.
They don't understand
The true dirt and grime,
Of life and how it is today.

Their world is full of bubbles
And they giggle with delight.
They're not drowning out their sorrow
They're not giving up the fight.

They're playing in the bath tub
In which I wash my soul . . .

> One of life's creations,
> So delicate and pure
> Playing in a bath tub.
> So innocent, so happy so sure

CLOSE THE CURTAINS

Close the curtains on the sun
Another day's begun.
Another day of loneliness
Another day of shame
Another day of misadventure
Full of personal gain.
> I'll sit in bars alone,
> Till 12 o'clock at night
> And meet a perfect stranger,
He'll be my husband for the night.
My loneliness is cured,
For another hour.
Yet when the curtains open,
Like a child I cower.

DON'T DO THIS TO YOUR CHILD

She sits upon the stairs,
Listening to the voices,
Listening to her mother,
Giving her father condemned choices.

'It's her or me you imbecile,
Make that final choice.
Pack your bags and go
Just leave me here in peace.'

Then everything goes quiet,
And she's left there in the dark.
Tears streaming down her innocent cheeks
She is alone. She is frightened.

She hides under the duvet
Clenching her brown bear
All her life goes into this
She doesn't think you care.

She wants to pack her bags,
Run away and hide
She opens up her window
And slowly climbs outside.
She leans a little further
To try and touch the sky . . .

You're still fighting,
You're still shouting,
You're not with her when she dies . . .

SILVER LININGS TURN TO RUST

They say every cloud has a silver lining.
What does it mean?
What does it matter?
If there is a silver lining,
And I've searched with all my might.
Is it covered by the rain?
Is it covered by the night?
Is it kept at bay by fog?
Has it given up the fight?
       I know I have . . .
If there is a silver lining,
High up in the clouds.
Is it protected by a sorcerer
Who conjures up great spells?
Is it hidden in a box,
With locks of mighty steel?
Or is it glorified so much,
That the silver is not real?
Is it just a cloud of rust
Slowly shedding its dust,
Over fields that lay fallow
Over children out at play
Over people sodden to the bones
With tears and nothing to say?
One day this silver lining,
Will be where I want it to be
Until that day the silver lining
Sheds its dust on me.

BELOVED IMMORTALITY

(On watching 'Interview With A Vampire')

You are my
Prince of Darkness
fulfilling my bloodlust desire.
I gave you
everything
for
just
one
taste
of immortality from
your lips.

I succumbed to your desire
as you breathed life into me
with poetic breath . . .

I fell from grace
knowing I could live forever
and taste other mortals'
passionate fear . . .

Knowing I would never
see the burning fire of life
or feel warmth on my glowing cheeks.

I am your Lady of Darkness
and together we take flight
to feed our
beloved
immortality . . .

SKIN-DEEP

Shop doorway:

Hidden by the adolescent scars
is a face full of pride.
Hidden under a mass
of unwashed
unkempt hair;
is someone
who could be happy.

Mutton dressed as lamb:

Hidden underneath a slab
of foundation and
60's eye shadow
is someone withered,
old and worn;
worry lines underneath
the eyebrows greying;
drawn on.
Hidden underneath the lipstick
a mother's thousand words
of unheard warnings.

Ethiopian child:

Hidden under the fresh
faced youth, of
the nine-year-old.
Is a mother
of a brother
a father to a sister
A carer of a grandparent;
cooking; cleaning;
washing; working.

Behind each face
lies a voice that's mute.
Stories which won't be told.
Ambitions never fulfilled,
wasted on growing old.
Their lives; incomplete;
their stories; skin-deep.

IN A CAGE WITHOUT BARS

She smiled,
He talked.
She listened, disinterested - but interested.

He shouted!
She smiled.
He got angry.
She ignored him.
He was screaming; he was hitting.
She was *hurting*; she was smiling.
He was kicking: Breaking every
Bone in her lonely body.
She was smiling, she was happy.
She was wanted, she was needed . . .

He abused her and he used her.
But she was smiling; *never* crying,
It *was* hurting; she ignored it.
She was loved . . .

SOULS OF THE OCEAN

We sit desolate, submerged in our bed of sand
not knowing the years that have passed,
our sails ravaged by the storm-fuelled tides.

Wood preserved to perfection
by our soul's salty heaven.
Skeletons oblivious to their graves
lay under fallen beams.
Their flesh feeding the
generations of fish-life.

A cabin-cruiser shines with golden glory
As the sunlight fades the morning mist
of silt clouds.

A fleet of Spanish sailing ships
lie cannonballed to driftwood
wearing seaweed dressing-gowns.

A war sub lost in battle
still holds a mother's child.

We creak and sway in the tide of emotion
and relish in the knowledge of isolation
knowing that your time will come
and you'll join the souls of the ocean.